the RESILIENCE WAY

Enjoy!

the RESILIENCE WAY

Overcome the unexpected and build an
extraordinary life...on your own terms!

Kelly Ann McKnight

The Resilience Way™

Visit us on the web at www.theresilienceway.com!

This book is dedicated to my four amazing children, William, Liz, Grace and Katherine. You keep me grounded with your unconditional love and steady support. You remind me that life carries on in sometimes unexpected ways and it's up to me to make it count, for myself and those around me.

Contents

This is a book about:

A little girl who learned to hold it all together no matter what,

A young woman who learned about love and found a beautiful life,

The amazing man she loves,

A woman and her children who survived and surprised,

A woman who carried on.

What I know:

1. The universe brings you what you need, when you need it.

2. You need to know yourself in order to recognize the things the universe is bringing.

3. Be real, be yourself, people will recognize your authenticity and respond in amazing ways.

4. This is not the endgame – this is only part of the journey.

5. When the world needs you, it's time to figure out how to step up.

6. There are good people around you. Be open to them. Notice them. Connect with them. Be curious about what your connection might bring.

7. There are people who take away your strength, intentionally or unintentionally. You need to manage your relationships with these individuals.

8. Be careful about your attachments to outcome. Learn to be aware of when it is a good thing, and when not.

9. Once you get clear about your purpose, don't doubt yourself. You are stronger than you think.

10. You will falter. That's okay. Learn from your mistakes and move on.

Chapter One

Our Stories

David's Story

It was standing room only.

The church had room for four hundred people, but today, late arrivals were left to stand in the back. At the front of the church stood the huge organ pipes and the choir area, but the choir was not present this day. Only the organist, there to play the hymns. A railing in front of the choir area separated it and the minister's podium from the rest of the pews. Dozens of hockey sticks lay against the railing, placed there by some of the young people attending the service.

This was the funeral service for a forty-five-year-old man. A husband, father, brother, son, friend – and hockey coach. He had lived his life with quiet selflessness and had died embracing that same approach. He would have been amazed at the turnout, never understanding the deep impact he had on those who knew him.

It was a celebration of his life, a life lived well, and with amazing resilience.

Only two people spoke during the service; Kate, his minister and spiritual leader for the past few years, and his widow. Kate had been directed on the structure of the service by the man before he died. His widow had been working out the details of his eulogy for many months, perhaps years, really. Both women were following through on promises made to this lovely man.

His name was David, the Hebrew word for "beloved".

David was a remarkable man for many reasons, but the most prominent and most often noticed reason was that he was who he was, without complication. He never tried to be what he was not. When you met him you immediately noticed his strength of character and his sense of humour.

Most people connected with him quickly and learned to appreciate his candor, as well as his constant teasing. If he liked you, he teased you more. He was a man full of good, sound advice, always given with the person's best interests at heart – and whether requested or not, usually appreciated. The world was straightforward for David. He used his intellect – he was very bright – and his common sense to sort out people and situations. His analysis was usually "bang on". Many learned to rely on his judgement and if we ignored his advice, it was at our peril. He would often meet someone and know immediately that they were not trustworthy. He would eyeball situations or ideas and know right away what would work and what would not. He was usually right.

David's strong sense of character and common sense was deeply rooted in his childhood and being raised in a rural community with strong agricultural roots. He spent his summers happily working on the farm and learning that hard work pays off and nothing worth having comes easily. His life was not easy, but when he and his sister Rhonda were still in grade school, the divorce of his parents and the family issues that followed left significant scars. Although his childhood was complicated, he was blessed with love and affection from parents, siblings, a wonderful granny and one very special aunt.

These individuals taught him many things, including resilience.

As with many people, the struggles David endured during his childhood gave him the strength to handle other challenges later on. As a new graduate from university, David landed a great job with a bank, where he worked hard and enjoyed many promotions throughout his eighteen years there. When there were no new challenges at the bank, he moved on to a new opportunity with another company.

Meanwhile, at home he was farming, raising four children, coaching them all in hockey, and keeping his wife happy. He did all of these things with great success.

In June 2009, David's life took an unexpected turn.

David had been in his new job for ten months and all was going well. He turned forty-two on the Saturday before Father's Day. He lay on the couch most of that day with what he assumed was the flu. He got up in the late afternoon and attended a dance recital for his oldest daughter, but still was not feeling well. The next day, Father's Day, and he decided to go to the emergency room to see about this flu. He was concerned about missing a conference he planned to attend on Monday, with his wife in tow. It was an annual tradition and much anticipated get-away for the two tired parents.

David called his wife around noon from the hospital. They were concerned about some blood test results and were going to keep him a bit longer. Later, they admitted him with what they thought was diverticulitis. He was given an ultrasound and a cat scan. On Wednesday, late in the day, the surgeon came to the hospital room to share the news. The scan showed a tumor in his colon and lesions on his liver. It looked like stage-four colon cancer. There would be a consult with the cancer centre in order to figure out the next steps.

That was a terrible night.

David and his wife spent many hours crying and gasping for air. The words that had come from the surgeon's lips seemed surreal. The situation seemed impossible. Surely, someone would come along and explain that there had been a mistake. But no one did.

Eventually, David's wife went home and tried to sleep. She returned early the next morning; having been away about six hours.

9

Now, this is the resilience part. Get ready. Here it is...

David was sitting up in bed and greeted his wife with a smile and a kiss, and then said, "Dr. Anderson is on her way in this morning. I want to talk to her about next steps."

No more tears, no more "why me?", no more "this can't be happening". He had taken several steps toward accepting his new reality and wanted to get on with discovering what was next. This should not have been surprising. David had always lived his life according to a set of values that included putting his family first, and dealing with situations with a practical, logical approach. This new reality was no different for him. Overnight, he had decided that nothing could be gained by feeling sorry for himself. So, he also decided to do what needed to be done, nothing more. He felt responsible to be strong for his family and friends, as they went through this process with him. He was ready to take on the future, no matter what the future brought.

That is resilience!

"The way in which a man accepts his fate and all the suffering it entails, the way in which he takes up his cross, gives him ample opportunity – even under the most difficult circumstances to add a deeper meaning to his life."

Victor Frankl,
neurologist, psychiatrist, holocaust survivor and author of
Man's Search for Meaning

The following day the surgeon did a scope and sent away a sample, which confirmed that the tumor was malignant. David was sent home to await further instructions.

At the first meeting with the oncologist, David was told that he had at least one year to live; and at most, three.

The next three and a half years were spent living with cancer. David endured chemotherapy every two weeks for most of that time. He spent two days of every cycle with a bottle attached to his side that administered the chemotherapy drug. He carried it on his belt in a little bag intended for a water bottle. He took it to the hockey bench as he coached, to work and to bed. He treated it as if it was completely normal – and so it was.

That's resilient.

David had a colostomy installed during a surgery that removed the tumor from his colon. He accepted the colostomy in stride, and it became a source of both stress and humour. Stress when it filled at inopportune moments (you don't get to choose when it fills, or the noises and smells that accompany it). Humour when he would revert to his eight-year-old boy bowel talk, but with a whole new level of fun.

The lesions on his liver were too extensive for surgery and the hope was that chemotherapy would shrink them to a point where surgery might be possible.

That never happened.

Chemotherapy kept the lesions at bay for almost three years. Several clinical trials of new drugs had some effect, but in July 2012, David was told that everything that could be done, had been done, and that he would be gone in three months.

11

What he did next was typical of the resilience with which he lived his life.

In his common sense, selfless way, he asked for a notebook, so he could make a list.

He made a list of the contacts his wife would need when he died. He listed his employer's human resources person, the insurance company contacts, the banking contacts and the minister's information. In each case, he listed their names, telephone numbers and any details that would be important. He checked on the process that would need to be followed upon his death and made notes. He called the township and arranged the purchase of a burial plot. He dragged his wife around to look at the local graveyards so they could choose the right one. He also dragged her to the local gravestone supplier, and then sat and planned his gravestone. He did not trust that his wife would be able to get this task done once he was gone. He was probably right, as usual. He had a meeting with the minister, Kate, to plan his funeral service.

He did not plan the hockey sticks, they just arrived.

My Story

David was my beautiful husband.

I grew up in suburban Toronto in a middle-class neighbourhood where the kids all played outside together. In fact, it was a cul-de-sac, which meant that we had little concern about cars and the street was basically just part of our play space. All the houses on the street were relatively similar, though not in the cookie-cutter style of today. It seemed that families had slightly bigger or smaller houses based on the number of kids they had inside. Everyone seemed to have "enough" but no one was particularly wealthy.

Our house was popular because we had a pool in the backyard. The entire gang of kids used to swim all summer in our pool. We would alternate swimming with spreading our towels out on the black driveway to warm ourselves in the sun. No one wore sunscreen in the summertime, and we were never burnt, because there was still an ozone layer that protected us. It all seemed so blissful.

In my house, however, there was a significant lack of bliss at times. Depending on the time of day and, more importantly, where my father had spent his afternoon, our house could be a funhouse or not.

Sober, my dad was funny; sometimes even goofy. He was creative; an artist and musician. He was the life of the party. He was a business consultant by day and that meant that he routinely met with clients in bars and restaurants, where they had lunches that lasted until evening. If he spent his day in a bar somewhere, he then drove home to continue drinking throughout the evening.

When drunk, my dad was a verbally and emotionally abusive jerk. You would avoid him if you could. It was often unclear what might create an "upset" that would trigger his abusive side, so we walked on eggshells trying to stay out of his way.

I was often away in the evening, as I was a competitive figure skater and trained several nights a week. It was my brother who was left at home with our dad, and he still bears the scars from that exposure.

I learned to pretend, in the outside world, that everything was fine at our house. It was not hard, as my dad went to work every day in a three-piece suit, drove an expensive car and most people only encountered him when he was either sober or only somewhat intoxicated. I was a star student and athlete, and if you asked me what I wanted to do when I grew up, I would certainly tell you I was going to be a doctor. People thought we were good, in the same way that I thought everyone else on the street was in better shape than us. It was only in later years that I began to realize that others were also dealing with issues.

I recall a particular night, when I was thirteen, and my dad arrived home at about five-thirty in the evening. I remember the time so clearly because when he came inside in a rage, it was because an outdoor light had not been left on for him. We tried to explain that it had only become dark in the last few minutes, but his switch had been flipped and he launched into a tirade of verbal abuse. This reaction was par for the course, but I had had enough. I began to yell at him and ended by telling him to get out of our house and leave us alone. He laughed, saying that without him, we would not be able to survive. I assured him we would, and repeated my demand that he leave. To my surprise, he did! My brother and I were stunned and elated.

We turned to our mom and asked her to have the locks changed. Her response was stunning to me then and still rattles my sensibilities today. She said she did not want him to leave, because that would "uproot" us. She explained that if they separated, we would have to sell the house and move into an apartment. We readily agreed that this would be fine; we would happily live in an apartment if it meant not living with this tyrant. She disagreed.

My dad stayed out all night, but was back in the morning. I learned a few critical lessons that night, but had many more questions than answers.

Several years later, my dad did move out. He and mom had lived separately in the same house for many years, and in the meantime, he had met another woman. We had met her and really liked her. She was a lot like my mom. He moved into an apartment and we stayed in the house. I am so grateful that, within the year that followed, my dad and I established a new relationship and were on good terms. We did not work through any of the upset and he was certainly still drinking, but we were able to be civil.

I can't imagine how much harder it would have been if we were not talking when he died in a car crash a year later.

Feelings about my dad are confusing. I used to feel angry that he was not around. At times, I think about how much he would have enjoyed my farm life and my children. But then I realize that if he were alive, he would probably still be drinking and I would not have allowed that around my kids. I guess we will never know what might have been.

By the time my dad died, I was in my last year of high school. I left for university the following year and was really only home for short stints after that. I met David as soon as I got to university and we became fast friends. Six months later, we fell in love – and the rest is history.

When I look back on my early experiences, I notice all the people who were around to help me.

15

My mother has been a strong support throughout my life, and as a child, I was always aware that she put the needs of her children ahead of her own. She sat at rink side while I skated, unless she was working her extra part-time job to pay for my ice time and coaching. She made it clear that I was capable of achieving whatever I wanted. She also set the expectation that I would go to university and become a doctor.

Research shows that the most important factor in determining who will attend university is whether or not their parents attended. In my case, the fact that my mom did not have the opportunity to go meant that she was bound and determined that I would. And so, I did.

There were several other important characters in my childhood, including two strong grandmothers who showed me that with hard work and ingenuity, you can make things happen.

One of my grandmothers was frustrated with her two daughters, who were fighting over the position of the covers on their shared double bed. When they went to school one day, she sawed the headboard, mattress and box springs in half to make two single beds. Apparently, the saw broke halfway through the box springs, so she took the bus to the hardware store to get a new blade. By the time the girls came home, they had separate beds. Now that I have kids, I can better understand the frustration that would inspire this story.

Nevertheless, she was a force to reckon with and taught me a great deal about life.

My father's mother, who I also loved dearly, taught me an interesting mix of lessons. She was a deeply religious woman with some odd contradictions to her story. For instance, she had been forced to get married because she was expecting. In 1939 this must have been no small matter. I have long wondered if my grandfather was even the father of her baby, as there seems to be little resemblance. My grandfather was such a sweet man, I wonder if he just did what seemed right. My grandmother then lived a devout life and preached everywhere she went. I recall her telling me as a young child that if I behaved well, and followed the rules of her church, I would get into paradise. She also made clear to me that my mother would not be in paradise with me, because she did not follow the correct path.

Even as a youngster I saw the nonsense in this story that had my mother, who spent all her days trying to keep her children safe, going to hell and my drunken father joining the rest of us in paradise. So, from an early age I knew that adults did not always have all their ducks in a row.

But I also respected my grandmother's devotion. She had dedicated her life in service to God. I loved going to services with her and learning the bible stories. I loved the people we met at those services and the community they had created.

It was many, many years before I would find that again in my life.

What I Learned from My Grandmothers

1. If you think you've got it bad, think again.

2. No one is going to hand you anything. If you want something, get to work.

3. You only need three dresses, one for church, one for school, and one for play. There is no real benefit to having so many more.

I learned a number of critical lessons in my childhood experience.

I learned that you don't have to accept your current situation and that you can push back if people interfere with you. I learned that I could be successful at the things I wanted to do, despite challenges. I grew to believe in the idea that I had already experienced some tough stuff, which gave me courage and confidence. When faced with difficulty, I would think, "I've faced worse than this and survived, so this is unlikely to take me down."

That belief held true until the day of David's diagnosis.

Lost

Stand still. The trees ahead and bushes beside you

Are not lost. Wherever you are is called Here,

And you must treat it as a powerful stranger,

Must ask permission to know it and be known.

The forest breathes. Listen. It answers,

I have made this place around you.

If you leave it, you may come back again, saying Here.

No two trees are the same to Raven.

No two branches are the same to Wren.

If what a tree or a bush does is lost on you,

You are surely lost. Stand still. The forest knows

Where you are. You must let it find you.

David Wagoner

Chapter Two

Why Resilience

The Journey to The Resilience Way

Throughout the time when David had cancer and continuing after he was gone, people kept saying things I did not understand. Doctors and nurses would say, "You two are incredible. I can't believe how well you are handling this." Or they might say, "If I was in your shoes, I would not be able to handle this so well." These comments were always confusing, because I saw nothing in our behavior that was extraordinary. As far as I could see, we were just carrying on, and I became curious about other peoples' curiosity. I wondered why they were so surprised.

It took me a long time to begin to understand what was happening. People did not think they could have handled it all as well as we did. I kept thinking they would though, that surely, if they were faced with our reality, they would do the same thing. Eventually, however, I began to notice that this was not true. I realized that many people could not handle a diagnosis like David's in the way David did. Many people would not have the coping resources he had developed. In fact, many wouldn't handle lesser struggles with the resilience David demonstrated so brilliantly.

I am blessed to be able to share this resource of resilience with others, in the hope that it might help them cope with their struggles.

We had a situation handed to us and we were dealing with it as best we could.

21

During our cancer journey, we had low moments and happy moments. We saw some successes and we made some mistakes. But mostly, we carried on living and trying to raise our children in what we knew was a difficult situation.

We also knew the situation was only partly in our control, and so, we tried to focus on those parts. We gathered the best information we could find from the experts around us. David did everything the medical experts recommended and asked them good questions to make sure he fully understood their recommendations.

We always had hope that we would get through the cancer journey and come out the other side, so that we could grow old together. At least until the day David asked for the notebook, and then made his final list, the list that he knew I would use after he was gone.

When David was diagnosed, I could not see any option other than putting one foot in front of the other, and carrying on. We had four children to raise. At diagnosis, our baby Katie was only four, Grace was seven, Liz was nine and William was twelve. They were little. They needed to continue their childhood with as much happiness as possible. They needed to feel that their lives were secure, and that whatever happened, they would be okay.

That was our job. It was plain and simple.

As David's wife, my job was also to make him happy. He was my rock and now it was time for me to make sure he could remain stable and strong. I'm not talking about outward appearances, what other people saw. I did not care if people saw him feeling emotional. That was fine. My concern was for his internal strength. I needed him to remain positive and confident about his life and the lives of his family. He needed to see that I expected him to survive, that I had hope.

As time went on and the situation worsened, that hope changed from expecting survival to expecting more time. We had hope for another Christmas together.

David died on October 3rd.

> Hope doesn't mean you know something is going to happen, just that you are committed to wishing for it. Hope is a choice. It is resilient.

In the aftermath of losing David, I began to think more about what other people were noticing about us. I wondered about what made us remarkable to others. I decided it was because we managed our difficulties better than anyone else expected. People have expectations about how others will act and react when faced with struggles. When facing a diagnosis, at age forty-two, of stage four colon cancer and a prognosis of three years to live, you are expected to fall apart. You are expected to feel sorry for yourself and to struggle to carry on with your life. Feelings of hope and joy are not what others anticipate for you.

And yet we had so much hope, and we continued to find joy in our lives as we raised our children, continued our work and found time for one another.

People seemed so surprised by our behavior. It took me a long time to figure out why.

They recognized that they would have struggled more in our situation. That they were not dealing with their current struggles, which they considered less onerous than ours, as well as we were.

It was not a competition, but I do think that David's struggle was more serious than the issues most of the people around him faced. Yet he was happier and more "together" than many of the people he knew. This was really confusing for people.

With time and contemplation, I can now see that there was a significant difference, and I now know that difference to be "resilience".

We had some very specific things present in our lives that allowed us to be resilient. We had the support of one another and of many wonderful people. We had a clear purpose and understanding of what we wanted to accomplish. We also grasped and accepted what was and wasn't in our control. We did not waste time or energy worrying about things we could not change. We remained positive and confident in our abilities to manage through the tough times.

It was not by chance that we were resilient. We had ideas that allowed us to put elements in place that helped us when we struggled. The point of this book is to share these ideas, in the hope that they will help others.

The Resilience Way is based on years of research and learning in the area of resilience. There are many books and resources with the word "resilience" in their title, most are nothing like The Resilience Way.

For the most part, when others talk about "resilience" they are referring to psychological resilience. They focus on elements of managing emotions, creating the right mindset, and being mindful or "present" in the moment. All of this is part of The Resilience Way, but there is much more.

It is clear to me that there are additional pieces we all need to put in place. These are things like relationships that support us, clarity in terms of our direction, and/or habits that support our physical health.

The Resilience Way recognizes that we need a range of "Elements" that support us when times get tough. In fact, we will look at five Elements in detail before we are through. We need all of these in order to prepare ourselves and create true resilience.

That's "The Resilience Way".

I have been living "The Resilience Way" throughout my life. As the child of an alcoholic, my future might have been precarious, but I had a vision for my life going forward and the confidence that I could do whatever I wanted. I learned to solve problems and keep myself on track. I was gifted with strong relationships, including a very determined mother who instilled in me a sense of confidence and determination. There was really no other option than to find my success. As a result, I have rarely taken the easy or common path. I have taken the path that made sense to me and have not shied away from following the difficult path. By doing so, I have accomplished what I wanted and built my resilience along the way.

Throughout my adult life, my work and conversations with the amazing people I meet, have allowed me to learn about resilience. As a Management Consultant and Executive Coach, I have had the opportunity to work in the realms of management and leadership development and have coached many leaders. I have watched people cope with difficulties at work and at home. I have observed amazing leaders and those who struggled to find success. I have watched people dealing with minor struggles who seemingly fall apart in the process. I have been blessed to meet many people who have successfully worked through significant challenges and grew as a result of the experience. The difference between those who succeeded, and those who did not, was resilience.

The ability to face struggles, big and small, and take on struggles of our own choosing, in order to move us forward on our chosen path, depends on our ability to hone our resilience.

The Resilience Way is based on both my life experience and my research into resilience. I have looked at many models, concepts and theories covering how people manage their struggles. I have explored the elements of resilience and figured out what makes a difference for those trying to build their resilience. As a result, The Resilience Way is a model and a method that will allow you to take steps to build and improve your ability to find success in your life, despite adversity and challenges.

The Resilience Way Process

If you choose to dive into this book, you will go through a learning process that can help you develop your resilience. You have already begun this process, just by opening your heart and mind to the stories and concepts shared so far.

Storytelling is a critical part of The Resilience Way. It is a powerful way to share, learn and inspire. I am grateful to all those who shared their experiences, telling their stories in detail or adding to supporting data for the model by sharing what factors impacted their experience. From the stories of many others, we can learn which factors and behaviours can allow us to move through our difficulties to find growth and happiness. The stories come from ordinary people, just like you and me. They have encountered struggles in their lives and have worked through them.

We can begin to understand that there are a specific set of skills, abilities and a mindset that those who are resilient share. No one is perfect when it comes to resilience, but some definitely have stronger resiliency than others. They move through tough times and come out the other side with strength, growth and happiness.

Each of these stories has something to teach us as we try to increase our own resilience and lead full lives on our own terms.

Throughout this book you will hear more of my story, David's story and our combined stories. We had many struggles together and many opportunities to demonstrate our resilience. You will also hear stories about how all of our lives moved forward after David died. The kids continued to learn and grow, and a man named "George" entered our lives and became my new husband, and step-father to the kids.

It's been an eventful journey and the stories help to demonstrate how key resilience has aided our continued growth as individuals and as a family.

In addition to learning from stories, you will also learn about the specific model that is The Resilience Way. You will learn about all of the elements that make up this method of building and developing resilience.

As part of this learning process, you will have the opportunity to complete a self-assessment of your current resilience strengths and weaknesses. This will allow you to approach The Resilience Way with an eye for what you want to improve and areas of strength you already possess.

At the end of the process you will build an action plan that will allow you to implement the learning. In this way you can ensure that The Resilience Way becomes a tool for making real and long-lasting change in your life.

Overall, this book is a hands-on tool to help you notice your resilience strengths and work on developing elements that will lead to increased resilience.

And that, is The Resilience Way!

Resilience Defined

Before we dive into the elements of The Resilience Way, we should spend some time considering the concepts behind the model. I also want to be clear about the scope of The Resilience Way and what it can, and can't, accomplish.

Let's start with a couple of definitions for resilience:

"…capable of withstanding shock without permanent deformation or rupture."

Or

"…tending to recover from or adjust easily to misfortune or change."

These are dictionary definitions of "resilience" and though they're useful, they are limited in scope. The first one relates more to resilience in terms of physics, not human emotional well-being. The second one ignores the potential for growth that is possible when we successfully survive our struggles. Neither definition considers that we all need to maximize our emotional well-being, while navigating our struggles.

In other words, life goes on while we deal with difficulties and struggles. For many of us, the struggles we face will take months or years to work through. In the meantime, our children need to be raised, bills need to be paid, and we need to find joy and happiness despite our difficulties. We can't put our lives on hold while we sort through major issues, nor do we want to.

"I don't mind suffering. You suffer in all things — work, relationships, whatever else you do. Unless you're eating ice cream, you're suffering."

Jerry Seinfeld

The Resilience Way includes a number of assumptions that are inherent in the model. It is worth taking note of some of these assumptions:

1. **Shock and Resilience**

   If a shock or trauma initiates our struggle, that event may prevent us from wholeheartedly pursuing resilience. Transitioning away from this stage, so we can begin applying our 'resilience muscles', needs to happen quickly, but we may find we have little control over this process.

2. **Contentment and Hopelessness**

   We will seek and must find ways to maximize our **contentment** and

29

minimize feelings of **hopelessness** or desperation. This is a process over which we have some control. We must also understand that managing contentment and hopelessness will be an ongoing process as we move through our struggles.

3. **Growing from Struggle**

   We can and should grow as a result of difficult experiences. These life struggles provide the kind of 'education' that allows us to develop tried-and-true resilience, which results in new strengths and expanded levels of confidence about our ability to manage future struggles.

4. **Defining Success on Your Own Terms**

   We can build strength by purposefully taking on struggles of our own choosing. These targeted difficulties help us learn to trust and better define our reactions to struggles. Thus, we can accomplish what we want, meeting no one's expectations but our own.

Let's have a closer look at these assumptions and how they relate to The Resilience Way.

Resilience and Shock

When we think about our resilience, we are considering the skills we possess to deal with struggles AFTER the initial shock wears off. We would never want to criticize or even critique ourselves, or others, in terms of how we handle those initial moments.

When you hear about a diagnosis, endure the unexpected loss of a loved one, or receive other shockingly bad news, you just react. It is not useful to be concerned about reactions in those moments, as they are too raw to allow behavioral choices. Be kind to yourself in these moments. Wait until you feel ready to move forward before attempting to do so.

You do, however, want to move beyond the shock as quickly as possible so you can begin to make choices and decisions about your situation. People who lack resilience might stay in that state of shock and their feelings of helplessness indefinitely, being unable to move on.

And it's important to move on. Resilient people will move on as quickly as possible.

David was a crazy example of this. We received his diagnosis of probably stage four colon cancer at the end of the day on a Wednesday. We lay in the little hospital bed together for many hours. We cried. We were in total disbelief. We simply did not know how to make sense of this news.

Late in the night, I went home to try to sleep, but did not. I arrived back at the hospital early in the morning to find David sitting up in bed, smiling. His first words were, "Good morning, my love, I'm just waiting for Kate to come and tell me what the next steps are going to be."

He had moved through the shock and was ready to hear about the plan for moving on and through this terrible situation. I was shocked by his mood, as I was not feeling as "put together," but his mood lifted mine. We met with Kate, our wonderful family doctor, later that morning to talk about next steps.

In this situation, David demonstrated his ability to transfer his resilience to others. His strength in this moment was an inspiration to me, and allowed me to feel more confident and hopeful than I would have otherwise. In this way, resilience is shared and spreads.

Now, let's be real here... David did have more moments when the shock returned and he did struggle with the disbelief of it all. But each time he quickly moved back to "What do I need to do about this?" He maintained his emotional well-being by focusing on what he *could* control, instead of feeling like a victim or wondering, "Why me?"

Contentment and Hopelessness

In many ways, resilience is just common sense. I often think there is a severe shortage of common sense these days, but some parts of The Resilience Way are just that. I look around and I see people struggling with things that were, not so long ago, not issues at all. I meet people who feel a hopelessness or a sense that things will not get better, and don't have the energy to make change happen.

We struggle with finances; and in some cases, it's just because we don't have a clue how to handle money. We create financial woes by spending more than we make on things we don't need. We pass our time "connected" to people online, but not making any real connections at all. We measure our relationship success by how many "likes" and "followers" we have, and yet if we really need to talk to someone about something important, we may not have anyone who will take the time to listen.

We spend our time and money in ways that do not support our happiness, nor do they build resilience.

In my grandmother's day, you fed your family on a tiny budget, you lived in a house just big enough for your family, and you lived within your means. You had the support of your friends and neighbors when you ran into trouble. People knew what was going on with their community and came together to share work. In rural communities, there were "barn raising bees" and church suppers that built strong communities. People worked, and then they rested. Kids played, and did chores around the house and farm.

In the old days, people suffered from depression and anxiety, but not in the numbers that they do now. People were more active and ate simple, healthy foods. It seems like their lives should have been more stressful, but I think they were less stressed.

According to one study:[1]

> "American culture has increasingly shifted toward an environment in which more and more young people experience poor mental health and psychopathology, possibly due to an increased focus on money, appearance, and status, rather than on community and close relationships."

Now, we have stuff, debt and stress. We shop constantly and fill our homes and storage units with stuff we don't need. We work at jobs that don't feel fulfilling, in order to pay off the debt accrued from buying the stuff we don't need and our expensive homes and cars.

At the end of the day, we are not happier. We are not more content.

We are all so busy and are so accustomed to being busy that we don't know how to stop the madness.

We are stressed. We feel that things are hopeless. We are no longer resilient.

Luckily, we can absolutely make changes to our lives and our habits and see reduced stress and increased feelings of hope and contentment. We just need to create clarity about what really matters to us and begin to align our behavior to this new understanding.

We can rediscover our "common sense".

> There are, by the way, no short cuts in building resilience. Beware anything that seems like one.

My favorite example of today's consumers trying to find the fast-track to contentment can be seen in any home decorating store. Head on in and you will see the words "Live", "Love", "Laugh" and "Hope" painted on canvases, etched into wood, or ready to attach to your walls in myriad ways. Then you can head on over to the clothing store and grab a t-shirt with these same "slogans". Or perhaps a mug?

Beware these items, or more importantly, the idea behind them. They suggest that we should be able to easily focus on these things and all will be well. My concern though, is that most of us have little to no idea of how to bring these things into our lives. Nor do we know how to sustain them. I also fear that, for most people, these words become a reminder that they are not achieving these things.

If I just start laughing, will that change everything? I do love to laugh. And maybe, for a few minutes, I might feel good if I watch something funny or talk to a friend and share some giggles. But in the long run, I'm not creating real change.

Perhaps it would be better to create your own resilience plan and hang it on the wall. My wall plaque would say, "Eat fruit, Exercise, Stay Centered." If I did those things more consistently, I would maximize my "Live, Love, Laugh & Hope" quotient.

Your plaque would be different. It might say, "Create your Vision" or "Don't Forget Your Personal Boundaries". It would be based on whatever you need to improve. Over time, your plaque would change – mine, too. I'm getting better at making meditation a constant in my day, so I might be able to take that off one day. Whatever it expresses, our plaque needs to stay current.

> We need to recognize that building resilience is an active journey.

You get better by making changes, not just hoping for them.

Life is not all about being happy, either. Let's be clear… if you think that you should always be happy and that any time spent not happy is somehow not okay, or that perhaps unhappy times are times of lost time – you need to re-think.

> A resilient life involves being present in the moment, no matter what is present for you in that moment.

In Western society, we focus on happiness as if it is the goal of our lives. I think that mindset is guaranteed to bring on a whole host of problems. If you see happiness as your only goal, then you will not struggle to achieve difficult goals. Instead, you will avoid situations that need to be resolved, because the process won't make you happy. You may even begin to think that you have a "right" to be happy and will be prone to self-pity when you do not feel happy. I wonder if making happiness your ultimate goal might be the best way to ensure that you are *not* happy in the end.

Growing from Struggle

We can't go back to being someone we were before any struggle. We need to let go of that person, that prior state, and be willing to move forward.

I remember asking my dear friend, who had also lost her husband to cancer, when this disease would stop being a constant part of my thoughts. She said that after over a decade, she was still very focused on cancer and expected that she would never go back to her pre-cancer state of mind.

I think I had spent most of my life avoiding the topic of cancer. Now, it's a part of my reality, in both positive and negative ways. I worry much more than I ever did about being diagnosed. I also know that early diagnosis can be the difference between living and dying; and that the journey through cancer is tough, but manageable. I have definitely grown as a person through my experience. That's resilience.

Resilient people recognize that they have built their resilience through experience. The old adage, "what doesn't kill you makes you stronger" resonates for resilient folks. We know we are better, stronger, and more confident and that we can and will endure because we have in the past. We have a track record of success that shows both survival and growth. We are better than we were before.

Our goals should be about building resilience so that we can live a full life, living up to our potential. Being resilient allows us to deal with the struggles that arrive in our lives and invite in the struggles that will allow us to accomplish our goals. When we are resilient, we are not fearful of things we know will be difficult. We won't shy away from tasks, projects, or life directions that we know won't be easy. Instead, we will take a deep breath and say, "Bring it on!"

Defining Success on Your Own Terms

There are loads of books, webinars and online courses on topics like "attaining high performance" or finding "success" or "power" or "wealth". We seem to respond to these calls to action to become rich and famous, and live our lives as though what others think matters.

I was recently invited to a presentation called, "How the World's Most Successful People Fit a Day's Work Into 2 Hours." I feel that most people I know are struggling with much more fundamental issues than figuring out how to do more in less time. If you feel disconnected from your life goals, and don't feel in control of what is going on in your life, doing things faster is not going to help.

Tools that help you do a job you hate faster, so that you can do more of that job you hate in any given day, are not going to solve your problem.

Many of us need to change what we are doing entirely. We need to develop clarity about what we want to be doing, so that "work" is not something you try to fit into the shortest time possible.

The Resilience Way is about doing what you love to do with passion, focus, and contentment. It's about following your dreams, whatever they might be, and overcoming the issues that you find along the way. I don't try to do my work faster, because I love what I do and it takes the time it takes. And that's not a problem.

This book is not about becoming "the best" in the sense that you should be better than everyone else.

> Resilience means being your authentic self and becoming whomever you feel compelled to become.

In order to do this, you have to have a decent understanding of yourself – who you are and what you want in your life. I know this makes sense because I watched David do it. He died with no regrets because he lived his life on his own terms. That's rare, but entirely possible.

According to Bronnie Ware[2], an Australian nurse who spent years working in palliative care with patients in the last twelve weeks of their lives, similar regretful themes surfaced again and again.

Most often, she found that people had regrets over:

1. Not living a life that was true to themselves and their dreams.
2. Working so hard and missing out on time with family.
3. Not expressing feelings and allowing bitterness and resentment to build up.
4. Not giving their friendships the time and effort they deserved.
5. Not pursuing choices that would lead to true happiness, and instead, sticking to old habits and fearing change.

For most of us, these five regrets have one thing in common, they are all driven by our need to live our lives according to someone else's rules. They involve meeting the expectations of others, but not our own, and not building and maintaining relationships that really matter. We might be meeting the needs of family or colleagues or society in general, but not our own. Perhaps we are doing what someone in our position "should" do. Sometimes, this is fine. Sometimes, it is unavoidable. And sometimes, it gets in our way – especially if we are unaware we are doing it. We can avoid these regrets with self-awareness, authenticity, and the confidence to live our lives according to our own rules.

Finally...

This book is intended to help you figure out what works for you, and how to use those things to gain a life without regrets. There is no guarantee of fame and fortune. There is no attempt to make you "the best", unless that is your absolute calling.

For most of us, all we want is to live a good authentic life, enjoy the gifts we receive, and work through the struggles in a way that helps us grow…and that's all.

> "You'll seldom experience regret for anything that you've done. It is what you haven't done that will torment you. The message, therefore, is clear. Do it! Develop an appreciation for the present moment. Seize every second of your life and savor it."
> Wayne Dyer

Chapter Three

The Model Overview

The Resilience Way Model Overview

Based on my research and my life experience, both at home and in my work, I have developed a way of thinking about resilience that I now call The Resilience Way. This model is based on five elements, or areas, we can focus on in order to improve our overall resilience.

You will find that, in some areas, you already possess abilities and strengths, while in other areas, you need improvement. Below are the five elements:

The Five Elements of Resilience

Emotional well-being involves being in tune to what you are feeling and why you are feeling that way. We need to learn to tune into our overall emotional state and create awareness of what is going on. With this awareness, we can start to deal with issues, look for support, and learn about the triggers and obstacles that seem to get in our way.

This requires introspection and a willingness to wonder about and dig into your emotional state.

The element of emotional well-being is about taking care of your mental wellness; and not ignoring problems when they arise. You must not fall into the trap of believing that mental health is a taboo topic. You must view your mental health as you do your dental health: keep a close eye on it and get help when you need it.

Resilience requires that you have a reasonable level of mental health. When we ignore the signs and symptoms of mental and emotional issues, we don't allow ourselves to be resilient.

Emotional well-being also involves spirituality. We can gain a great deal of strength, peace and hope through our connection to our spirituality.

Now, spirituality is not religion. The resilience benefits in spirituality come from feeling connected to the universe and that our existence involves more than what we can see. The benefits from resilience come when we feel more emotionally grounded as a result of our spirituality.

44

You may have come to this understanding through a conventional religion; however, many will find that their spirituality is not connected to any religion, and that is fine.

Relationships have been an important, if not essential, element in the lives of human beings from their beginning. We were never intended to live independent of one another and are tribal by nature. We need to be in relationships with other people.

Resilient people enjoy strong relationships that help them through the tough times. In fact, tough times build relationships, because the shared experience builds connection between people. When you successfully survive difficulty together with others you create stronger bonds to one another. To grow our resilience, we need to look for support from others, and then enjoy the feelings of comfort and stability that come with that support. We also need to use the people we trust for feedback and advice when we need it.

The viewpoints of others can offer insights that we may not be able to see on our own.

The act of helping others is also a key action of building resilience. We can enjoy the rewards of feeling that we are useful to others and the benefit of knowing that we can help others. This giving-and-receiving builds our relationships through trust, knowing we can rely on others when we need them – and that they will return the favor.

Finally, we need to notice any relationships that are actually, or have the potential of, reducing our resilience. We may have people in our lives who are difficult, destructive, or even abusive. We need to deal with these people by constructing boundaries that protect us. These boundaries might involve changing our reactions to these people and what they do. If this is not possible, we may need to change or even end the relationship.

Personal clarity is essential to becoming and remaining resilient. To establish this element means having a clear picture of who you are, what you want in your life, and how you plan to achieve your ultimate goals.

This practice involves being clear about your values and determining what absolutely must be present in your life for you to feel comfortable. When you understand your values, you can notice when situations are not in line with them and react accordingly. Your vision, the ultimate picture of what you want to achieve in your life, must also be clear so you can be and remain aligned to this vision. You also need a clear set of personal goals with pre-planned steps that move you toward your vision.

Without this personal clarity, you will be pulled in directions that clash with your goals and values, and in tough times, you will have a hard time making good decisions.

It may seem that in crisis all this planning goes out the window, but resilient people use this clarity to steer them through the storm. Adjustments to the plan might be made, but awareness of the plan ensures that these adjustments are in line with who we are and what we want in our lives.

Once you have clear direction, you are ready to move forward.

Dynamic thinking is the concept that allows you to move forward with resilience, some skills, and a mindset that will enable you to implement your plans.

First, you need the confidence to know that you can and will succeed.

Confidence is about optimism, to the extent that you need to be able to see the possibilities in front of you, and not be pulled down by any possible risks. You also need to be able to see situations realistically, so you can notice what is getting in your way. And finally, you need to be able to learn to adapt to situations and change your habits and behaviour when they get in your way.

Resilient people can adapt and change in order to accomplish their goals. They are not, and do not get, stuck in old patterns that are not working.

Your **physical health** is the final piece of the resiliency puzzle.

As anyone who has been seriously ill can attest, if you don't have your health, you have nothing. Although this statement is simplistic, it is basically true. As resilient people, we need to maintain our physical health in order to be able to play in the other areas of resilience.

In order to achieve our personal goals, we need to be healthy.

Now, we don't always get to control our physical health, and many can tell stories about how their health became an enormous struggle. But even in those times, we want to separate what we **can** control from what we can't, while working on maintaining and improving our physical health as best we can. We can do this through good habits in the areas of sleep, nutrition, and exercise.

The Overall Goals of Each Element

All of the elements bring us benefits in terms of improving our lives through resilience. Each one brings something different and they work together to create The Resilience Way.

Here is a run-down on what each element brings to the table:

1. Emotional Well-Being

You need to be able to manage your emotional well-being and feel supported in your connection to the universe.

2. Supportive Relationships

The deepest need of human beings is to feel connected. You need to build relationships with other people in ways that support your needs and theirs.

3. Personal Clarity

You need to know where you are going in order to have any chance of getting there. Be clear about what matters most to you and what you want to accomplish in your life.

4. Dynamic Thinking

Change is a constant and things that worked for you in the past may not work in the future. You need to problem solve and be able to adjust as you go.

5. Physical Health

Your body is your tool for moving your through life. You need to maintain it and deal with any issues that arise.

The Resilience Way Factors

As you read on, you will discover that each of the five Elements are further broken down into three "Factors". These factors are the detailed parts of The Resilience Way, where we can discover which specific behaviors and mindsets need to be resilient. This higher level of detail is where the 'rubber meets the road' and you can start to see what is truly working and what is not. At this point, you can also build your specific action plan for improvement.

The figure on the next page provides an outline of the **five Elements** and **fifteen Factors** that make up The Resilience Way. The book will dive into each of these areas in detail to help you fully understand the concepts.

For example, if you struggle with maintaining your emotional well-being, it will impact your relationships. Perhaps you are feeling depressed and, as a result, you stop seeing your friends. They may think you are busy or disinterested. Over time, they may stop checking in with you. Without the support of others, it will be more difficult to improve your mental health.

There is also a positive cycle we can tap into, as we improve in one area (supportive relationships, for instance), other areas will follow along (in this instance, your emotional well-being). We need to learn to harness these opportunities and take advantage of the linkages between the practices.

EMOTIONAL WELL-BEING

Self-Awareness · Mental Wellness · Spirituality

SUPPORTIVE RELATIONSHIPS

Seek Support · Support Others · Boundaries

PERSONAL CLARITY

Personal Values · Personal Vision · Planning

DYNAMIC THINKING

Confidence · Realism · Learning Focus

PHYSICAL HEALTH

Sleep · Nutrition · Exercise

Overall, The Resilience Way describes a complex, interrelated system of elements. We can increase our resilience by learning about and building skills around the elements that help us when we struggle.

As you read this book, you will:

- Learn much more about The Resilience Way and what it takes to develop each of the Elements.

- Dive into the five Elements and learn about the three Factors that make up each Element.

- Have the chance to measure your resilience with The Resilience Way Assessment Tool.

- Be encouraged to write a specific action plan, which will help you make real change in your life.

This is an opportunity to learn and reflect, then implement the learning and make significant improvements in your resilience and your life.

In the next section, you will have the chance to measure your current state of resilience and gain some clarity about what you need to do. This will help you to focus, as you read about each element, identifying which are your strengths, and which are areas for development.

Chapter Four

Measuring Your Resilience

Your Current Resilience Elements

Resilience, by the way, is learnable.

Thankfully, resilience can be learned at any age, so if we aren't born with a full complement of resilience elements (no one is), we can build and attain them like we would any skill. You can learn about the elements of resilience, and then start to improve the areas you think are weaker. You can learn how to capitalize on your strengths to help develop skills that eventually balance your resilience.

A necessary part of learning about your resilience strengths and weaknesses is to complete a **resilience assessment**. I have developed just such an assessment, which will give you a clear picture of your resilience in terms of the five critical elements of The Resilience Way.

By completing this brief assessment, and considering your personalized results, you will have a better understanding of your strengths and the areas that need improvement.

Be as honest as possible, as you consider your responses, and remember: everyone has areas that need some attention. Resilience is not static and flexes with the situations and demands of your life.

You have two options for completing your assessment: online at theresilienceway.com or complete the version below and score it yourself. Either method will give you identical information you need on your current resilience.

Your assessment results become your starting point for developing your resilience over time.

55

In the final chapter of this book you will develop an **action plan,** which will take you from where you are today, to a higher level of resilience.

The Resilience Way
Self-Assessment

In the column marked "Score" in the survey below, enter the number that corresponds to each question based on the following scale:

1	2	3	4	5
Never	Rarely	Sometimes	Often	Almost Always

Question	Score
1. I stay focused on the present or the "here and now".	
2. When I'm feeling upset, I can recognize how this impacts my emotional state and actively find ways to work through it.	
3. I focus on taking care of my mental health as part of my overall wellness.	
4. I am comfortable seeking professional advice or a support group for help with my mental health.	

5. I feel connected to a higher power or to the universe in a meaningful way.	
6. I feel connected to a community/group of people who share my spiritual viewpoint.	
7. I accept help and/or advice from others when it's offered.	
8. I search out people who have experience or resources I need and ask for their help.	
9. I help others, without any expectation of reward or recognition.	
10. If someone asks me for help, I readily offer what I can.	
11. I identify people and relationships that are not helping me to be strong and happy.	
12. When I find a relationship is reducing my strength and happiness, I take action to deal with this person/relationship.	
13. I can clearly articulate the three most important values in my life.	
14. Considering my personal values, I behave in ways that are consistent with these values.	
15. I can clearly articulate my overall vision or purpose in life.	
16. I align my decisions to my overall life vision, and I try not to allow others and/or circumstances to move me away from my vision.	
17. I have set a clear plan for my next 5-10 years.	

18. I can articulate steps that I will take in the next three to six months to implement my plans.	
19. When I encounter obstacles, I feel that I can work through them.	
20. I can look objectively at my fears and find ways to overcome them.	
21. I consider what is and isn't working in my life and determine what needs to change.	
22. I seek information and feedback and use it to determine how to improve myself or my situation.	
23. Once I decide that I want to make a change, I can alter my habits accordingly.	
24. I recognize the emotional triggers that send me back to my bad habits and I use this understanding to make lasting change.	
25. I feel rested each day.	
26. I am aware of and follow good sleep habits.	
27. I maintain a healthy weight, according to my body mass index (BMI) or some other standardized measure.	
28. I focus on eating well by following current nutritional recommendations.	
29. I am physically able to do the activities I would like to do.	
30. I follow an exercise regime that is appropriate for my age and abilities.	

Scoring Your Assessment

Combine the scores for the questions indicated under the "Add" column Then, enter that sum in the blank box under "Scores". The maximum score you could have received in each case is next to your entry. The fourth line is the total of the three **Factor** scores and also your total for the **Element** being measured. At the bottom of the assessment, you can sum all five Element scores to create your **Overall Resilience Score**.

Element	Factor	Add	Scores	
				Max
Emotional Well-Being	Self-Awareness	Q1 + Q2		/10
	Mental Health	Q3 + Q4		/10
	Spirituality	Q5 + Q6		/10
Total Emotional Well-Being	(Sum all 3 Factors)	Total		/30
Supportive Relationships	Seeking Support	Q7 + Q8		/10
	Offering Support	Q9 + Q10		/10
	Boundaries	Q11 + Q12		/10
Total Supportive Relationships	(Sum all 3 Factors)	Total		/30
Personal Clarity	Personal Values	Q13 + Q14		/10
	Personal Vision	Q15 + Q16		/10

	Planning	Q17 + Q18		/10
Total Personal Clarity	(Sum all 3 Factors)	Total		/30
Dynamic Thinking	Confidence	Q19+ Q20		/10
	Realism	Q21+ Q22		/10
	Learning Focus	Q23 + Q24		/10
Total Dynamic Thinking	(Sum all 3 Factors)	Total		/30
Physical Health	Sleep	Q25 + Q26		/10
	Nutrition	Q27 + Q28		/10
	Exercise	Q29 + Q30		/10
Total Physical Health	(Sum all 3 Factors)	Total		/30
Your Overall Resilience Score	(Sum all 3 Elements)	Add all scores in shaded boxes		/150

Interpreting Your Results

When you have completed your assessment, you can see your overall scores for each **Factor** and **Element**. Keep in mind that, at this point, you have not learned much about The Resilience Way, so some of this will not make much sense – yet.

That's okay.

From here, the book will take a deep dive into each section so that you can better understand the details. We will come back to your scores when it's time to do some action planning.

For now, just take note of your strengths and your areas that need improvement. This way, you can think about them as you read and move forward in your learning. You have probably already discovered that you have some clear strengths. This is great news, because these will support you as you try to develop new skills and make improvements where needed.

Now, let's dive in!

Chapter Five

Emotional Well-Being

EMOTIONAL WELL-BEING

Self-Awareness · Mental Wellness · Spirituality

The first Element of Resilience we will explore is **Emotional Well-Being**.

This is the element that helps us to be centered in our understanding of our thoughts and feelings. It also creates a foundation for the other elements.

This element involves three Factors: **Self-Awareness, Mental Health and Spirituality**.

Self-Awareness involves being in tune with what you are feeling and why. It is about being in the present moment and managing your reactions to people and situations. In this factor, you will learn about some concepts and ideas that help you to maintain your strong emotional state or to begin to improve your situation, if you are not feeling emotionally well.

Mental Wellness demands an honest discussion – no shying away from it. You will learn to deal with problems and how ignoring the signs and symptoms of mental health issues can keep you from being resilient. Learning to be aware of your mental health status helps you maintain and grow your resilience in this area.

Spirituality is the factor that helps you to understand your connection to the larger universe, in whatever way makes sense to you, and gain support from that connection. When you establish this, you can enjoy the knowledge that you are not alone.

Self-Awareness

What is Self-Awareness?

> "He who knows the universe and does not know himself, knows nothing."

This great quote from 1679 by the famous French poet and author Jean De La Fontaine sums up the idea behind this topic. He is also known for the many fables he wrote, including "The Hare and the Tortoise", a book most certainly about resilience.

For our purposes, **Self-Awareness** is "the ability to recognize and manage our feelings, emotions and related behavior." You understand your emotional triggers. You can also see how other people see you. With **Self-Awareness** you can learn to control your emotions and your reactions to people and situations.

How Self-Awareness Builds Resilience

Self-Awareness is a critical step in being able to manage your resilience. If you can notice what is happening with your emotions, you have the critical feedback you need to manage them. With this, you can understand the impact that your feelings have on you and your behavior and modify as needed.

The Self-Awareness Continuum™

Some people have learned the skill of **Self-Awareness**, and others have not. Some of us are somewhere in between. There is a continuum of **Self-Awareness**.

You probably know someone who seems to have absolutely no clue about what is going on with their emotions. You see their behaviour, perhaps they are quick to anger or become quiet and withdrawn when they encounter an uncomfortable situation. They seem limited in their ability to control their reactions to situations and people. They may even blame their issues on other people or situations, without taking responsibility for their own involvement.

You may also know someone who seems completely aware of their inner self and can control their emotions and reactions to situations and people. They have a grounded, centred approach and they can find space to be compassionate towards others. They take responsibility for their actions and reactions. They can also create boundaries and understand when the actions of others are not their problem. I recall one such person in my own life, who had a knack for sharing thoughts like, "Well, that sounds like someone else's issue."

The table on the following page allows us to explore **The Self-Awareness Continuum**™ further. It looks at **Self-Awareness** as an area for growth and development as you move from the left to the right across the continuum.

Emotional Well-Being

Unaware	Informed	Novice	Self-Aware
This is the beginning state for most of us. In this state we have no self-awareness nor any understanding of the concept.	In this state we understand the concept of self-awareness but have not developed the ability to use this learning.	As we move into this state we are beginning to use our self-awareness learning. We are choosing the strategies that work for us but we still have limited scope in our abilities.	In this state we are self-aware. We continually notice what is happening inside ourselves and have the ability to adapt our strategies to different situations.
No internal reflection	No internal reflection	Reflecting on what is going on inside ourselves	Consistent self-reflection
Unconscious of our feelings, emotions and related reactions	Unconscious of our feelings, emotions and related reactions	Becoming more conscious of our feelings, emotions and related reactions	Aware of feelings, emotions and related reactions
Not present in the "here and now"	Not present in the "here and now"	More often present in the "here and now"	Generally present in the here and now
Tend to have an inaccurate understanding of self	Tend to have an inaccurate understanding of self	Developing a more accurate understanding of self	Possess an accurate (and emergent) understanding of self
Sense of self is based on social or other bias	Sense of self is based on social or other bias	Noticing social and other bias and how it impacts our sense of self	Sense of self is true to own values and beliefs

Tend not to seek feedback from others	Tend not to seek feedback from others	Seeking feedback from others (perhaps only those with whom there is safety and affinity)	Openly seek feedback and use this feedback to adjust course where appropriate
React passively	React passively	Use some strategies to manage reactions in an active way	Reactions are based on conscious decisions that relate to an accurate sense of self

When we lack **Self-Awareness**, we can't see the opportunities to manage our stress or to even to realize we are creating stress and anxiety in our own minds. With **Self-Awareness**, we can build our ability to recognize stress and worry as something we can control and let go of; freeing us to pursue our goal of becoming more resilient. If we allow stress and anxiety to take over, we can't access the positive energy we need to push through the tough stuff.

Dr. Wayne Dyer[3] helps us understand the power we have to control our emotions, and the negative outcomes when we don't:

> "...there's no actual stress or anxiety in the world; it's your thoughts that create these false beliefs. You can't package stress, touch it, or see it. There are only people engaged in stressful thinking. When we think stressfully, we create reactions in the body, valuable messages or signals requesting our attention. These messages might reveal themselves as nausea, elevated blood pressure, stomach tension, indigestion, ulcers, headaches,

increased heart rate, difficulty breathing, and a zillion other feelings from minor discomfort to serious, life-threatening illness."

When Dr. Dyer talks about stress and anxiety in this way, he is certainly talking to those of us for whom these emotions are optional, as they are for many of us. The situation that Dr. Dyer explains in his quote, and anything I'm saying about managing these emotions, does not apply to those who are suffering from depression or anxiety disorders. These are serious conditions that require attention and will be discussed in detail in the next section of the book.

Part of how people get to the **Self-Aware** end of the continuum is through mindfulness.

Mindfulness requires that you be centred in a way that allows you to be aware of your reactions, and then choose to act or react in a way that fits with your values and principals.

People find different ways of achieving mindfulness, and we will talk more about this later in this chapter.

Investing time in becoming centered is one of the keys to Self-Awareness.

People who have **Self-Awareness** are able to live their lives according to the famous quote from the Greek philosopher, Epictetus:

"It's not what happens to you, but how you react to it that matters."

To Epictetus, events that are external are beyond our control, so we need to learn to accept whatever happens.

Individuals are responsible for their own actions and need to be in control of those actions. That sounds a lot like resilience to me.

Tom's Story

So, one day I met a guy in a bar.

Well, it's not like it sounds, someone told me he was "the most resilient person they had ever met". Obviously, I needed to meet him. He invited me to meet at a place called Ethel's Lounge. When I arrived, I found him on the patio sipping a cold beer. Seemed like a resilient guy already! He shared a story with me that was a combination of shocking and inspiring.

The story begins with the son of a banker.

Tom had moved about every two years throughout his childhood, as his father was promoted and transferred all over Canada. The final move, when his father was transferred to Wall Street, didn't include Tom. He could have gone with, and would have been eligible for a green card, but the Vietnam War was still on and he did not wish to be drafted.

So, he stayed in Montreal and lived the hippie scene for a while.

Eventually, Tom decided that it was time to do something with himself. He considered his options and his grade ten education and came to the decision that the military was the best way to go. He joined the Canadian Navy. He went through basic training and encountered all of the grueling experiences you would expect. We've all seen it in the movies, the drill sergeant screaming into the face of a recruit, the fastidious bed making, shoe shining and uniform prep, and the impossible physical drills. Tom survived all of this.

71

He was soon recognized as a high potential seaman and was asked to train to become a Clearance Diver.

Now, this term seems innocuous enough, but it is really the Canadian equivalent of the Navy Seals. These folks do the work the rest of us might not even want to hear about. It was sold to Tom as a chance to learn to dive, and to jump out of helicopters into the ocean, to do recovery work. That means that he would need to find and retrieve bodies.

Tom said "Yes."

He remained a Clearance Diver for several years, while his wife and child awaited him on land. Eventually, the sea life and time away took its toll on his relationship, and his wife demanded that he either get out of the Navy or get out of their marriage. He chose to leave the military.

His wife had also done some research and sent him to St. Mary's University in Halifax, Nova Scotia, where they lived, to see about getting an education. Tom was told that if he took and passed a specific university math course, he would be admitted to the school. He and several of his military peers took the course.

They passed and decided to go out to celebrate.

The evening of this "celebration" was relatively uneventful. The men sat in a bar and had some drinks. One of Tom's friends in attendance at the bar was a quadriplegic. When it was time to leave, Tom tossed his friend's wheelchair into the back of his car. The chair did not exactly fit in the trunk, so the hood was left open. Off they went. When they arrived at the university residence where the friend lived, they discovered that the chair was gone. It had fallen out along the way.

And so, the search began, first for the chair, and then, when that seemed impossible, the search for a replacement chair. Now remember, it is the middle of the night and this friend cannot get around without a chair. They went to hospitals and anywhere else they could think of, but had no luck finding a chair. Eventually, Tom delivered his friend to his residence room. It's now early morning.

It just so happened that at this time (1982) the Pan-Am Wheelchair Games were being held in Halifax, at St. Mary's University – exactly where they were. As Tom wandered out of the residence building, he ran straight into a wheelchair athlete he knew. When Tom explained his predicament, the man readily offered his basketball chair for Tom's buddy to use.

Problem solved. All good, right?

Nope.

Tom got into his car and began the forty-minute drive home from Halifax. He fell asleep. He recalls waking to the realization that the car was leaving the road and all he could see was a rock face. Next, he recalls the paramedics pulling him out of the car through the passenger door. He remembers trying to look at himself in the rearview mirror. The paramedic pulled the mirror off completely in order to keep Tom from seeing that half of his face was gone. He thinks that what woke him was the fact that in order to pull him out of the car they had to straighten a leg that was badly mangled. He was not in good shape.

Tom flatlined for one full minute in the ambulance. He was told about this later. He recognizes that he was dead for one minute.

He spent a month in the hospital recovering from his accident. He was eventually left with one leg an inch shorter than the other and a badly scarred face, despite the skin grafts and attempts to repair it. He was apparently facially disfigured enough that a potential employer later said that he "had great qualifications, but they would not know where to put him."

Can you imagine? But I'm getting ahead of myself...

73

Once Tom recovered, he did start that degree at St. Mary's. He did a five-year degree in three years. He had become an expert in information systems. By the time he finished, he had two children, but his marriage was still in trouble – and it did end.

Tom was on his own.

Tom moved to Ontario and began a successful career in Information Systems. He proved to be a strong leader and had the ability to inspire creativity and innovation in this teams. He managed many challenging systems mergers, and led many teams through daunting projects. Many people saw him as both a strong leader, and a resilient person.

I asked Tom about resilience, and like many other resilient people I've spoken with, he had never really thought of himself in that way. Yet it is clear to the rest of us that he has shown many signs of resilience.

He was yanked out of peer groups as a child and forced to leave old friends and make new ones every couple of years. He was deep into hippie culture and recognized both that he lacked direction and that the military would provide a stable space while he sought direction. He survived jumping out of helicopters to search for, and eventually pull out, dead bodies from the cold Canadian ocean. He lost his first marriage. And then, there was the crash and the recovery. Oh, and by the way, how many of us would be able to carry on when half of our face became seriously disfigured? Would you have the resilience to keep showing up to job interviews?

Tom has built a highly successful career, been a good father, and is a good husband to his second wife.

As I hear Tom's story and how he talks about his experiences, I can see that the element of Emotional Health is strong. He has the **Self-Awareness** to realize how he is feeling and not allow his feelings to determine his behavior in the moment. He talks about having a personality that is quick to anger, but also about having the ability to notice this anger building and deciding not to act accordingly.

He also can recognize that he is having a bad day, and let it be just that, nothing more.

He describes his world view:

> "I can have a Loss of Identity Day, because of something that's gone wrong, perhaps a job loss or an upset at work, and I know it's going to feel bad. But a bad day today is not connected to tomorrow. Just because today I'm feeling bad does not mean I will tomorrow. But I also don't impose things on myself... I don't say I'm feeling bad, so I'm going to make myself feel better. I accept my feelings. I give myself the privilege of feeling what I feel."

Tom realizes that eventually his "bad" feelings – anger, sadness or frustration – will pass – and he recognizes that in the grand scheme of things, he's okay. He has a roof over his head and food on the table. He can think about things that make him happy, and this allows him to move on.

This is another interesting part of Tom's resilience: his ability to "move on" when the situation requires it.

To be honest, when Tom first mentioned that he had twice left good jobs when the organization made changes he did not care for, I thought he sounded like a quitter.

My first reactions were: "How did you know things would not work out?" and "Why not stay and see how it went?" But this is a key part of Tom's resilience. When something is not going to work, he moves on. He has an awareness of what is going to work for him and what is not. And when he gets to the point where it's just not worth investing more time and energy in the current situation, he has the courage to move on.

This story also teaches us about being willing to let go of situations; including jobs, relationships and plans that are not working for us. We can let go of our attachment to our plan when it is no longer taking us in the direction we want to go.

The social stigmas around being a "quitter" also need to be reconsidered, so we are not finishing things that should never have been started in the first place.

Creating awareness of how we feel about a situation is critical to our ability to make judgements about the best path forward.

How many people stay in a job or a marriage, even though they know it's not working and it's probably not going to get fixed?

Tom cuts his losses and moves on. In his words: "Why would I spend my life doing something I don't want to do, when I can change it?"

Why, indeed?

So, Tom's story teaches us about being self-aware. How are you feeling today? Accept that feeling as your own. Don't be attached to the need to change that feeling, as this might make things worse – especially if the fix does not come as quickly as you expected. Trust that you will work through your feelings, once you identify and own them. Just noticing them is the first step to resilience.

As we dive deeper into **Self-Awareness,** we need to look closely at the things that support or challenge our ability to become and remain self-aware.

We will look at the concepts of:

- Mindfulness
- Personality
- Happiness
- Gratitude
- Guilt
- Grieving

In each of these areas, we will look at what we can do to improve our overall emotional state so we can increase our resilience and gain the ability to move forward.

Mindfulness

"The past is gone, the future is not yet here, and if we do not go back to ourselves in the present moment, we cannot be in touch with life. Living mindfully and with concentration, we see a deeper reality and are able to witness impermanence without fear, anger, or despair."

Thich Nhat Hanh, "The Father of Mindfulness"

Nhat Hanh is one of the leading spiritual masters of our age. In his 91 years, this Vietnamese Buddhist monk has had a global impact as a teacher, author, activist, and the founder of the Engaged Buddhism Movement[4].

We all can benefit from learning to be more mindful in everything we do. We need to be more present in our dealings with others, more focused when trying to do complex tasks, and even more mindful when we are eating. How often do you wolf down some fast food without really noticing anything about it?

I sometimes get to the end of the day and think back to all the things I have eaten and realize there were several 'forgotten' trips to the pantry. That's not mindful eating. My mind was elsewhere while I gorged on crackers or cookies. It was certainly not my fully conscious decision to eat them.

When you think about all the people you worked with or interacted with in any given day, how many times did you really notice those people? Were you present for them? Did you help them in any way? Did you even listen well to what they had to say? How often are we on autopilot and not aware of it?

This is exactly how you can spend your life; doing stuff and never accomplishing anything you intended.

"Life is what happens while you are busy making other plans."5

I recently had the chance to talk about mindfulness with a dear friend, Jill Davey, who is a Hatha Yoga and Insight Meditation instructor and practitioner. Jill shared her thoughts about mindfulness and about the current attention the topic is enjoying in our popular media.

I'm sure you have noticed it... mindfulness is everywhere, and nowhere!

Mindfulness is a journey to becoming a better person, for the sake of the universe. The point of meditation is to create an awareness of your body in the present moment.

We do this by developing a practice of meditation that allows us to become centered and focused. Where we normally have our minds focused on the future or the past, we learn to bring our focus in line with our body – in the present. When we do this, we can become centered and more quickly and accurately aware of our feelings, from those that are upsetting to those that signal joy.

We need to develop a relationship with these feelings through being mindfully aware of them as they occur and accepting them. When we do this, we can begin to enjoy a calm that allows us to react more "skillfully" in all parts of our lives. We get better at managing our intentions and approaching situations with compassion.

In this way, we work toward the foundation of meditation, allowing ourselves to approach our lives with "wise speech, wise action and wise intention."

This is not easy and it requires help, learning and practice.

As Jill says:

"Most people are not trained to be mindful because it is not a mindful world."

The pace, the focus on materialism, and the attention to devices that pull us out of the present, keep us from being mindful. In order to counteract this, we need to find a teacher, we need to practice, and we need to let go of assumptions that "we can't do this."

Finding a teacher that you connect with is important. You need to learn about the foundations of meditation, and you need someone who can support you as you learn. You need to practice consistently, so that you eventually get better at finding your center and staying there for longer periods of time.

Be careful about your assumptions, too, since most of us think we can't meditate because we can't "shut off the noise" of our thoughts. The point of meditation is not to shut out anything, but to only notice thoughts and feelings, let them pass by, and then move back to center. In doing this, we develop an awareness of those distractions and can begin the journey of developing a relationship with them. We can then go further and develop a stronger understanding and intimacy with our own minds. We have then open up possibilities for increased compassion and empathy, both toward ourselves and those around us.

For many of us, the obstacle to developing our mindfulness skill is time. It feels selfish to spend so much time just on yourself. However, each of us need to recognize that this is not time spent on ourselves, but on the greater good.

> When you improve your own capacity for compassion, empathy and understanding . . . everyone benefits.

I encourage that mindfulness practice is good for us. I have struggled with this myself, but I do believe it is key to being present in our own lives.

Beware "Mindfulness Lite"

I have outlined the importance of mindfulness and mentioned that it is all over our popular media these days. Be careful not to mistake some of the tools that are out there for the true mindfulness tools that will bring you increased resilience.

I have used a couple of apps, for instance, that led me through ten-minute, guided meditations. These were lovely, but I'm sorry to say that they do not actually develop mindfulness. In ten minutes, you will feel more relaxed, but you will not have increased your capacity for compassion. You will not have changed your mind-body relationship.

You know the old adage, "Nothing worthwhile is ever easy." It applies here.

Sorry about that.

Resilience depends on our ability to notice what is really happening around us. A lack of mindfulness interferes with that. We need the mind-body connection that comes from mindfulness meditation. The awareness we can then develop is key to resilience.

When we are not mindful, we allow time to slip by without our noticing. Meanwhile, we are not living our lives with passion, focus and resilience.

Know Thyself

We need to be aware of what is going on in our heads and hearts when we are going through difficulty. This allows us to make choices about how we react, rather than just reacting. Very often the actions and reactions we take, when not being cognisant of our emotions, will not be those that are best for us or what we want. In this way, we can create issues and problems that don't help us work toward our overall goal, which is to have our behaviours driven by our awareness and resilience, rather than any feelings we have that pull us in different directions.

As part of my coaching and leadership development work, I use "personality style" to help people understand how their core personality influences how they relate to other people, as well as how they prefer to behave.

There are many tools you can use to explore your personality preferences, to get better understanding of your core personality. In learning these things about myself, I am better able to recognize my most natural personality traits and how they are helping or hindering me.

Sometimes, this leads me to change my behavior from the most natural approach to one that is more appropriate for the situation. In other cases, I might just find some forgiveness for myself when I am struggling with something that is really hard for me.

An example might be my organizational skills. I am not naturally organized. I don't even like to be organized. My favorite days are those that require no order at all…

I absolutely love a weekend day with no plans, no desperate tasks that need to be done, and no kids that need to be driven anywhere. It's a rare occurrence, but I love it. I love not having to plan and organize.

The reality, though, is that most of the time I am very planned out and prepared. In my work I have to be highly methodical. My workshops and coaching clients expect me to show up at the right time, with the right materials, to do my work. I can't just say, "I'm here, but I forgot the reports because I'm just not naturally an organized person." I would be out of business. So, I make lists, I double check everything, and I show up looking very organized. I do not forget, however, how difficult this is for me, and if I do mess something up, I have compassion for myself. I recognize that I'm not always going to get it right, because it is a true stretch for me.

An example tied more to my emotional side would be my constant need to be liked and accepted. My style is one where being part of the group is very important.

Now, as I matured into adulthood, I did learn not to let these basic needs interfere with my happiness. I learned that not everyone has to love me, only the people I love and respect. But that's still a big group. Again, I can continue to notice this tendency, I can watch for situations where it is getting in my way, and I can give myself a hug when I find that I'm falling prey to my "everyone hates me" side. I can carry on with the understanding that this is just my most natural tendency, and they don't have to define how I react.

> Understanding your personality style is a critical part of becoming emotionally aware.

These preferences also have enormous impact on our relationships, as they affect how we communicate and handle conflict with others. We can learn to adjust our behavior to improve our relationships, and we can recognize that some relationships are just going to be more difficult than others.

Difficult, by the way, can be wonderful – if you can bridge the "gaps".

One big "gap", or difference, between people is that some people tend to focus on the people side of things and others prefer to stick to thinking about the tasks or issues at hand.

For some people, making a decision that will have negative impact on people will be very difficult. For others, the most logical decision wins every time and they will figure out the people issues when it's time for implementation. If two people, one from either side of the gap, try to work together, they will not see the world in the same way. They may well struggle to see eye to eye. Neither of these approaches is right or wrong, they are just different. They both bring strengths and weaknesses.

> We need to recognize our natural preferences so we can understand our behavioral tendencies.

The other big differentiator between personality styles shows up as our interest or lack of interest in taking charge of situations and people.

Some of us, myself included, like to be in charge, and we struggle if we lose that control. We are always chomping at the bit to get involved in things, even if we were not invited.

I often tell my husband, George, a man with a PhD in physics, how objects should go together. I joke that there are laws of physics, but they adjust depending how much I want something to work.

If I build IKEA furniture on my own, I end up with a few leftover pieces, which I toss in the garbage. This would never happen with George as he would follow the directions carefully and make sure every piece was used. And yet, I can't sit back and let the poor man do any job without my "help".

You may be more like George, happy to let someone else take control of things, unless the task is clearly in your area of expertise or responsibility, and then you wish they would go away and let you do the job properly and without interruption.

You may enjoy a quieter style of being, where you can think inside your head and not feel compelled to share every thought that passes by. I have so much respect for those who bring a more thoughtful approach and can remain focused on tasks until they come to a logical conclusion.

Neither of these approaches is right or wrong, but can be appropriate or not, depending on the situation.

If a project needs some energy, my "get 'er done" attitude is appropriate. If I'm stepping on the toes of an expert, it's not. Not being as assertive can make you a good team player, but if you don't speak up, and let someone like me take over your project, don't blame me when it all goes south.

We need to recognize when we need to step out of our comfort zones and bring what is needed in the situation.

David's style was different than mine, and my new husband George's style is the complete opposite to mine. This is, by the way, quite normal. Many people marry someone opposite to themselves. This makes for a great blend of skills in your household; as well as some very difficult interactions.

I have found that the key to being married to someone very different from you is to recognize the parts of their behavior that are not easily within their control.

85

If I stop holding George responsible for his complete inability to multi-task, I can stop thinking he is being disrespectful. If George is working on something, there is nothing else going on in his universe. The proverbial herd of elephants could go through the room and he would not look up. The lack of ability to multi-task is the downside of a preference for extreme focus. The good news is that if you leave George alone for a bit, he sorts through all the data and comes up with a workable solution to almost any problem. This is a major upside for someone like me, who would rather not worry about the details. I have learned to "plant a seed" by explaining a problem I need to solve, and then I just come back later for the solution.

It's magic.

This understanding of other peoples' personality traits also helps with parenting.

All of my four children have different personality styles. Some are more different than others. These differences show up early and that's a sign that they are somewhat genetic in nature.

Katie, our baby, has a strong and determined personality. Her mantra from birth has been: *If the older ones can do it, so can I.* This was clear on the wintery day when I went outside to start and warm up the car before heading out with her on a trip. I was outside less than a minute. When I returned, she was standing in the hallway with her winter parka on. She was 18 months old. Her older siblings struggled with this task at five! She had watched them do it and figured it out on her own.

To this day, she remains the kid who has confidence and just goes about life assuming she can do whatever she wants. It's great. But, with that comes the frustration when things are not as she wants them. She can become angry and emotional if something or someone gets in the way of her plans. It's hard for her to "roll with it".

This makes sense though. You can't be intense in your determination and laid back when things get difficult. So, you must take the good with the not so good in your personality.

Katie will learn to be more patient as she grows and matures, but she will always struggle to balance these conflicting traits. My job as her Mom is to help her develop her patience, so she can celebrate her positives: determination and confidence.

Understanding your own preferences is important, so you can learn to value what you bring to the table, and to recognize what is going to create stress for you.

There are many examples of this in my life, including recognizing that my hopelessly positive outlook can keep me from looking at situations realistically. I just always think things will work out and am good at fixing the things that don't. I have to admit that sometimes it is better to see the potential risks in advance and do some contingency planning.

Our resilience lies in our ability to stretch our behavior in ways that meet the needs of the situation and allow us to accomplish our goals. There is no "resilient personality style", but rather there are resilient people who understand their own style and how it either helps or hinders them in particular situations.

There are several ways of coming to understand more about your own personality preferences. You can go to TheResilienceWay.com for more details. At the end of the day, you need to understand what your personality is like and how it drives your preferences in communicating, managing conflict, and connecting emotionally with others.

Happiness

According to the Buddhist view, well-being or happiness is defined as a deep sense of serenity and fulfillment, rather than just pleasure. According to Matthieu Ricard, the French writer, photographer and Buddhist monk, "this state of happiness actually pervades and underlies all emotional states, and all the joys and sorrows that come one's way." [6]

In this definition, happiness is a deeper sense of well-being, rather than a fleeting emotion. You can have this deeper happiness while also being sad or experiencing suffering in some way.

When we think of happiness as that fleeting "joyous" feeling, we tend to look outside ourselves for it. We compare ourselves to others and we focus on material things in our search for happiness.

Personally, I sometimes find myself with a strong feeling that... "I just need this one more thing" ... only to find that once I get it, I move on to wanting something else just as intensely. My wardrobe is a great example of this. I think I need a red jacket to round out my wardrobe, and then that jacket seems to need the right shoes. I will make extra trips to stores, searching for these perfect items that I could have easily lived without. And then, I complain that I have no free time. Sound familiar? This is how we end up shopping for things we don't need, planning for more and bigger houses and vehicles – 'living the dream'. We spend well beyond our means in an attempt to create this elusive happiness.

In the end, none of these things bring the kind of deep happiness we crave. We can't "find" happiness in all these crazy ways. We must learn to create happiness within ourselves. We think that happiness is something we "find" but in reality, it is something we make.

> "Happiness is not the absence of problems but the ability to deal with them."
>
> Harriett Jackson Brown Jr., Author,
> Life's Little Instruction Book

New research by Harvard psychologist, Dan Gilbert shows that our sub-conscious employs a system of cognitive processes that help us alter our views of the world, so we can feel better about situations that are uncomfortable or unfamiliar.[7]. We don't realize it, but we are changing our outlook so that we are happier with new situations and our lives.

Gilbert gives a great example when he asks us to choose between becoming a multi-million-dollar lottery winner or a paraplegic. The answer seems obvious, right? Or is it...?

It turns out that a year after either of these experiences, the individuals involved are equally happy. Research actually shows that gaining or losing doesn't tend to have an impact on our happiness. If you wait three months after a major life trauma, the vast majority of people will report no impact on their happiness.

How can it be that the paraplegic is as happy as the lottery winner? Or perhaps my question would be: "Why didn't we know about this this cognitive process until very recently?"

Had I known that the ability to create happiness was normal, I might not have been going to my counsellor shortly after David's death, asking her if it was okay that I was not falling apart. I was so concerned at that time that I found myself to be happy. I was convinced that I must be about to hit a proverbial wall. I was certain that I must be pushing my sorrow deep inside and that it would suddenly surface when I least expected. My counsellor was, fortunately, not surprised and gave me the confidence to trust that being okay was – well – okay.

Now, Gilbert's research shows that this makes perfect sense. With only a few exceptions, we create happiness soon after we process the initial shock of traumatic events. Happiness can be synthesized.

We need to recognize the strength of this psychological system and understand how it aids our emotional well-being.

We think the happiness that comes from winning or gaining something we really wanted is the best kind of happiness. Research is showing that the happiness we synthesize, based on accepting our current condition and situation, is just as real, and perhaps has greater impact on our resilience. If you don't understand or accept this happiness, then you suffer needlessly.

No matter what situation we find ourselves in, our brain is going to try to synthesize happiness.

In situations where we are hemmed in, where we cannot change our situation, we are actually great at synthesizing happiness. It turns out that having a lack of other options helps us focus on synthesizing happiness in our current situation.

Gilbert gives the example of the difference between dating and marriage. When you are dating, you consider your level of happiness with another person in the context of all the other potential suitors out there. When you are married, you tend to be happier with your choice of partner, because you are somewhat trapped in the situation. You find ways of making sense of your spouse's faults, because you have no other choice.

When we are locked into a situation, we find happiness in it.

We need to understand this idea and embrace this synthesized form of happiness. David showed us how. He was happy in his cancer journey. He never questioned this happiness. He embraced it. Of course, he had moments that were not happy, moments when he felt sad, frustrated and angry, but, for the most part, he was happy.

This was one of the things that confused other people I think, because it was unbelievable to them that David could be so happy, given his situation. This was the basis of the many comments about the "amazing attitude" or "surprising strength".

However, based on the research into synthesized happiness, it seems that David's emotional wellness was the expected psychological response. What was missing was others' understanding of this normal condition. Other people could not see past their own understanding of the situation, their thoughts of "I could never handle being sick like David is" and see that in many difficult situations there can be happiness.

I recall many times thinking about the fact that we were trapped in the situation of our cancer journey and had to "make the best of it". When people expressed their amazement at our resilience, I always thought immediately about the fact that we were short on other options. I often replied, "Well, we have four kids to raise and no other options with respect to the cancer thing. When another option comes along, I'm sure we will jump in that boat and sail off into the sunset. In the meantime, we will keep on keeping on."

And we were absolutely happy. I would have been happy to continue to care for my dying husband for the rest of my life.

Laurie Anderson

You may or may not know this name. Laurie is a highly acclaimed American artist, composer, musician and film director. She is also the widow of the musician, singer and songwriter, Lou Reed. In a recent interview, she shared her thoughts on loss, and in doing so, demonstrated her resilience.

She has a book out, *All the things I lost in the flood*, that shares her experience and learning after hurricane Sandy flooded her home in New York City in 2012. She describes how the Hudson River rose up, crossed the highway, and came up her street. She talks about watching the black water rise toward them. She and Lou spent the night sandbagging and were able to keep the water out of the house. The building behind the house, her studio, flooded. In the flood, she lost her entire physical archive. Within a couple of days, she was able to get to the studio and found that the sea water had turned everything into an "oatmealish brownish sludge". She recounted: "It was devastating. Everything was down there. Everything was completely gone."

Laurie's reflections on this loss, several years after the fact, are helpful. She has noticed that when people experience loss, they have to replace it, to find something better in order to make the loss bearable.

Laurie learned to be happy being unhappy.

She learned to find peace, despite loss. She also learned to be more in touch with her feelings and in understanding how she felt. She no longer finds it necessary to pretend she is not unhappy. She learned the lesson of **Self-Awareness** through the experience of losing things. Now she finds it really exhilarating to aspire to be in the present, not predicting what will happen tomorrow or regretting what happened yesterday.

As far as the lost archives, she shares her father's viewpoint. "When it comes to *stuff*, either you throw it out now or you throw it out later." Keeping "stuff" can drag us down and keep us from being fully in the present. When her husband Lou died in 2013, she donated his archives to the public library.

Gratitude

Gratitude is a critical part of resilience and a powerful emotion that we can learn to harness. Gratitude allows us to celebrate the present and be in the present moment. It allows us to appreciate the positives in our lives. When we are grateful we block negative emotions, and this can reduce depression. Grateful people are also more stress resistant, recovering faster from anxiety and stress. Gratitude allows us to strengthen our social ties and our sense of self-worth, as we recognize the people who have made contributions to our lives.[8]

According to Timber Hawkeye, author of the book, *Buddhist Boot Camp,*

"Gratitude turns what we have into enough."

He explains that gratitude is the antidote to any negative feeling you have. You can't be angry at someone and grateful to have them in your life at the same time. The moment that you are grateful, you can't be angry. You also can't be resentful or envious and grateful at the same time.

For those of us who struggle when our quick emotional reactions seem to get the best of us, a simple habit of gratitude can ground us back in the moment and a more positive state.

According to Psychology Today,

> "Practicing gratitude means paying attention to what we are thankful for, to the degree of feeling kinder and more compassionate toward the world at large. It can motivate people to make positive changes in their lives. Studies show that people can deliberately cultivate gratitude by literally counting their blessings and writing letters of thanks, for example. This proactive acknowledgement can increase well-being, health, and happiness. Being grateful—and especially the expression of it—is also associated with increased energy, optimism, and empathy."9

This quote really highlights the critical benefits of practicing gratitude. The resulting increase in well-being will help you take on whatever challenges come along.

Gratitude makes you more resilient.

Sandra's Story (Part One)

"But I have nothing to complain about."

My Aunt Sandra said this during a phone call not too long ago. The comment gave me pause. Her husband has had cancer and has undergone chemotherapy treatments and radiation. She has stage four lung cancer that was diagnosed almost a decade ago and she has undergone several rounds of different chemotherapy treatments. As one drug fails to work, they move on to another. Twice, she has been told they can do nothing more. The results have been mixed and the cancer remains present, but not growing … at the moment. Fingers crossed.

She has had to move from her beloved farm to a smaller home on the river, in order to set her husband up for carrying on without her. She has lost a beloved nephew, my David, at age forty-five to colon cancer. They shared their cancer journey for quite a while and compared drug side-effects and treatment plans. Those were strange conversations for an auntie and her much-loved nephew. Sometimes she lacks energy and feels unwell, but she continues to run the household and heads back to the family farm to do as much as she can of the chores. A dozen new calves arrive every spring…

…and she says she has "nothing to complain about." How can someone say that? Does she actually feel that way or is she just trying to be brave?

My best guess is that she has a level of confidence that no matter what happens, things will be okay. Throughout her life she has not shied away from challenges, and has taken on many of her own design, in order to accomplish what she wanted to do. When problems arise, and many have, she takes it all in stride and deals with them.

Sandra is grateful for what she has and feels the need to make good use of her talents. She does not "play the victim card", even though there have been plenty of opportunities to do just that. She finds creative solutions to problems.

Sandra's faith informs that there is something beyond this life and she knows her family is going to carry on. She has taught them well about how to support one another and how hard work will bring success. She knows she is strong enough to get through the rest of her journey.

Her thoughts, therefore, often turn to how she can help other people, and this becomes another source of her resilience.

Guilt

We all feel guilt. It is that feeling of dread that stops us in our tracks and helps us recognize when we have done something that is outside of or against our values. We are not born with guilt, but are taught it from the time we are children. This is helpful because it motivates us to fix our mistakes. Guilt helps us to live together in society with one another as we learn to understand when our behavior is hurting another person.

This is all fine. The problems arise when our feelings of guilt get in the way of our resilience.

> Sometimes we feel guilty for not living up to someone else's expectations and that can be a resilience issue.

We need to learn to ignore the guilt that comes from not living up to someone else's values and needs. Whether parents, partners, or others, we need to recognize when that guilty feeling is really a chance to notice how others are pushing your buttons, and to stop letting them do that.

An example of this happens to many of us with parents or other family members who have clear expectations of what we are supposed to achieve in life. Whether you are supposed to become a doctor, marry and have children, take over the family business – the feelings of guilt associated with not following others' dreams for you can be debilitating. Many people wind up doing what is expected of them, rather than what they are truly called to do.

This guilt, based on not meeting the needs of others, is certainly going to interfere with your ability to follow your dreams. Better to let go of these feelings of guilt, because left unattended they will reduce your resilience.

> If you have truly goofed up and made a mistake, the guilt you feel makes you want to do something about it.

Listen to that guilt. Pay attention to that guilt. Recognize that although perfectly normal, it is taking away your energy. You need to make amends, so you can move forward. If you don't, and I'm sure you have had this experience at some point in your life, the guilt will not go away. It might be twenty years later, but you will still feel this guilt. Best to deal with it immediately so that you and the other person can move on.

Another type of guilt that you might feel is "survivor" guilt, or guilt based on being better off than others. This can also be debilitating. You may well know of Retired General Roméo Dallaire, the Canadian responsible for the United Nations Peace Keeping Force in Rwanda in 1994, at the time of the genocide that killed six hundred thousand Rwandans.

Upon his returned from Rwanda, having witnessed unthinkable atrocities, he noticed:

> "Even the fact that I still had a family, when I had seen so many destroyed, felt wrong to me. Similarly, I shied away from non-work social engagements: too many friends I'd made in Rwanda had been slaughtered. I suspect that veterans of any mission experience some or all or even more of this when they return, becoming distant, introspective, unwilling to open up, mistrustful of themselves and others. At last I understood why my father's generation spent their post-war years on barstools in Legion halls. At least there they were understood, and so allowed themselves to be themselves—their new selves."10

A friend of mine who recovered from a serious cancer diagnosis, against all odds, felt survivor grief as she tried to make sense of why she had survived when so many others did not. She struggled with her sense of unfairness. However, she found that her guilt propelled her forward into making a difference by sharing her story, in order to reconcile why she survived. In this way, she dealt with the guilt that might otherwise continue to bring her emotional upset. I'm grateful to be able to share her whole story later in this book.

Depending on your life experience, you may have learned a couple of tricks for NOT dealing with guilt, allowing issues to drag on and on. You may have learned to repress your feelings of guilt, trying hard to ignore them, rather than dealing with the issues that cause them.

Another strategy we use is to "project" the guilt onto someone else. We will do something wrong to someone, and then instead of dealing with the guilt and fixing the wrong, we try to blame the other person. When we lay the blame on the victim, we don't deal with the guilt. I have done this when I quickly get angry with someone, and often without real cause. I will continue to see the other person and their behavior as the issue, rather than admit that I got angry too quickly and should just apologize.

Both repressing and projecting guilt fail as strategies because they cause you to fail to live in the present, and rob you of the relief you will feel when you deal with the guilt.

Instead of ignoring or putting your guilt onto someone else, try having a close look at what is causing you to feel guilty. Talk to a friend, family member, or therapist about your feelings. Try to sort out what is going on and what you could do about it to bring about a better result. Try journaling; writing down your thoughts as a way of getting them outside of yourself, where you can see them more objectively. Perhaps just allow yourself to write without worrying about what is coming out, and then leave it for a day or so before returning to re-read and learn from your thoughts on paper. This may well give you a new understanding of the situation, and from there, you can figure out a strategy for moving forward.

> It's all about moving forward rather than letting our guilt hold us to the past.

If you don't deal with your guilt, eventually it's associated negative feelings will bubble to the surface and interfere with your life. Much better to deal with the issue that is making you feel the guilt and be free of it, allowing you the energy you need to focus on your life goals and plans. No matter the type or source of your guilt, you will want to have a close look at it and how it is affecting your resilience.

Grieving

I think it is high time we have a broader understanding of grief and allow individuals the space and time to deal with their grief in whatever way makes sense to them.

The term "grief-stricken" is a good place to start. For me, it encapsulates the way most people expect to grieve. As a widow, it also frames the expectations others have of you, in that you are supposed to be absolutely "taken down" by grief.

You may be "stricken" or you may be "deeply centered" in your grief, as I was. Owning your own grief state and process is an important part of your resilience.

I have read many books and articles about grieving. Some were gifted to me by friends, others I found on my own. They all had something to share. None were more helpful than Thomas Attig's book, *How We Grieve*. Attig takes a hard look at grief and our grieving processes[11], including stories and research from other experts. His insights align with my grief experience, and the experiences many others have shared with me.

He describes our lives as a "web" and the loss we have experienced within the context of that web:

"...our resilience resides in what is not broken. To be sure, our daily lives are shattered, our life stories disrupted, our connections to larger wholes threatened or undermined, and our ego's illusions undone. Yet much in the tattered web of our life remains intact. Much good in the web of webs that has supported us throughout our lives remains available. And neither our soul nor spirit is broken. The home-seeking and meaning-seeking drives that animate our lives, though shaken, can and do address our brokenness and overcome our sorrow. Resilient souls find sustenance in familiar surroundings; draw from roots in family, community, history, and tradition; care and love deeply; and find faith, and courage to rise above suffering; stretch into the new and unknown; change and grow; seek understanding; and open to joy again. And the love that still pulses in our soul and spirit can cherish precious memories and lasting legacies, revive connections with fellow survivors, and open to new relationships. As our unbroken and resilient soul and spirit do these things, we relearn how to be our selves again in life in separation from our loved one."

This way of thinking about loss and grief always made sense to me. It fits with my experience. Attig describes the loss of a loved one as a trauma to the web, breaking some

101

of our connections, so that we have to rework the web and reconnect things.

I imagine my own web as having a permanently damaged spot. But, just a spot. The spot where David belongs. He is still in my web, just not in the way he used to be.

My grief work has been to rebuild my web in a way that it works, despite the permanent hole. The hole is not going away. It belongs there. To pretend or believe that it will go away is not respectful of the loss of David. He lived. He loved me. And his loss will always be with me.

Meanwhile, I am tasked with going on, with relearning my life, and finishing our parenting work we began together. And so I pull my web together, which still holds so much love, happiness and joy, and make sure it stays strong. My rebuilt web has room for new relationships, but these have no impact on the empty space left by the loss of David. It just exists. I respect that space. I pour my endless love for David into that space, and when I do, I feel his love return from it.

You don't stop loving someone just because they are no longer alive. Your relationship continues, just in a new, and at first, unfamiliar way. The job of grieving is to allow that unfamiliar feeling to become your new normal.

Tip: Learn to Cry

Go for the big, gasping cries that take hold of you. Find a place to be alone with your blubbering if you prefer, but don't avoid crying. Learn to trust that the waves of emotion will not take you down but will cleanse you and bring you peace.

Having explained the author and model of grieving that I love and that served me well, let me also explain some of what I did not find helpful.

Between the advice of friends, family, and acquaintances, and some of the more simplistic reading I did, I found lots of ideas that were not so great.

Some psychologists, for instance, simplify the grief process into "stages" or "phases". They will lay out a pathway, such as:

1. Acknowledge the Loss

2. Express Emotion

3. Learn to Live Again

4. Let Go

This particular pathway is attributed to William Worden, but there are others that sound similar. Again, the list flies in the face of my experience. If you had asked me, in the early days after David died, to "acknowledge the loss", I might have punched you in the face. There was no lack of acknowledgement. Other than the sacred moments after I awoke in the morning, when I was blissfully unaware that David was gone, the reality of his leaving was so real that it was constantly with me. So, no problem with that stage. Check.

And how about the last point.

Worden describes this as: "Loosen ties to the deceased. We must free ourselves from our bonds to the deceased in order once again to become involved with other persons. We must find effective means to say good-bye."

This idea is ludicrous to me.

> My bond to David has zero impact
> on my ability to "become involved
> with other persons."

In fact, I really wonder what this actually means at all. Does it relate only to romantic "involvement"? I certainly can still make new friends despite the loss of my husband. If it does relate to romantic relationships, then I still find that it does not fit my experience. As strange as this may sound to those who have not been where I have been, my new marriage, and the love I feel for George, exists in the same space where I still love David. There is absolutely no conflict in this. My love for George has nothing to do with my love for David.

Although Worden's pathway looks great on paper, and it probably sounds great to someone who has not suffered a significant loss, I don't find the idea of a staged process true to my experience, or the experience of anyone else, for that matter. We don't follow a simple path. Nothing about grief is simple. At the very least, when you look at these stages or phases, we need to recognize that, as a mourner, we will sometimes experience them all at the same time, and will also go back and forth through the process.

Point number three, "Learn to Live Again", is the only item on the list that really resonates. This is the work of grieving. This links back to the "web" model I love. My work has been to make sense of my life in a new reality, without David present in the normal sense. I had to make sense of how to carry on with the tasks of running a family, a business, and a farm, on my own. I had to learn how to have friendships with people as a widow, without David's involvement. I had to sort out a new life plan, given that continuing to look after David was no longer an option.

All of this work was made easier by my constant feeling that I was not alone, that David was never far away, that his love was there to support me. I reworked the web that is my life and found places for all the pieces it needed to hold. It took time and effort, and confidence.

I mention confidence because I did find that there were people and situations that seemed to want to derail my work. There were social expectations, complex relationships, and other constraints that made the job of relearning my web difficult.

The fact that there is a specific role for widows to play, for instance, did not help.

I found that even in this day and age, there are expectations around what a widow should and should not be doing and feeling. I'm so glad I had the confidence to ignore this. I know that I was supposed to be a blubbering mess, hardly able to get out of bed, but I wasn't. I know that I was supposed to be constantly sad, as if there was nothing left in my life that brought joy. Again, I ignored this, and went about town with a smile on my face.

I recall running into an acquaintance who looked at me in bewilderment, trying to reconcile my response to the question, "How are you?" I had said, "I'm great, thanks." That's how I felt that day. Perhaps happy to be alive. Happy that the kids were doing okay. Comfortable in the feeling that David's presence was always close by.

I giggled as I left this woman with a confused look on her face, because I know David would get a kick out of her reaction. She just didn't get it. You can be feeling the loss of someone so strongly that it consumes you, and you cry your heart out for five minutes, and then a few minutes later, you can smile and fill your grocery cart with food for hungry teenagers. It's just life. You just do it.

I ignored the clear expectations of people who did not understand, and thought, "Someday, I'll write a book about this, so others can find their way more easily."

It was like this also when I met George. I knew that folks would think it was too soon, that I was rushing. I wondered, in my less resilient moments, if they thought I loved David less because I was dating only eighteen months after his death. I wondered if they thought I was even capable of making these decisions. Remember the old adage: "Don't make any major decisions within the first year after you lose your spouse." It's as if there is something wrong with your brain; and therefore, your ability to make decisions is miraculously lifted on the first anniversary of your loved one's death.

It's ridiculous.

But in my resilient moments, which was my norm, I trusted that I knew what I was doing. I trusted that my love for George was real and healthy, and that it had nothing to do with my love for David. It all made sense to me. I knew it did not make sense to many others, including George. I recall specifically stopping myself when I was about to explain to George the concept of loving both of them at the same time. I was sure George would think that I was not ready to be in love with him, if I still loved David. He, after all, was certainly not still in love with his ex-wife, from whom he was recently divorced. So, I kept quiet and trusted that in time he would understand. And he did.

During the year or so that followed, George learned to live with the reality that David has a place in our family. He had a dream once that David spoke to him and asked him to care for his family. *His* family. Yes, we have become George's family, but David's love is still all around us. Before George asked me to marry him, he went to David's grave and asked his permission. He sees David's ongoing presence in our lives. It's not a problem. It just is.

I encourage anyone who is grieving, from a recent or past loss, to find the emotional awareness you need. Spend some time wondering about your web, and how this loss has created broken places in your web.

Then, think about how you can relearn your life so that you rebuild that web. What is missing? Who or what do you need to add to your life web? What help do you need? There is no right or wrong. There is no pathway that you are incorrectly following. There is no marking scheme that tells us if we are going through the process well, or not. There is just life, loss, and making sense of it all.

That's your job.

Don't listen to others who think they have it all figured out. Their web is different than your web. Have the confidence to believe that you can move forward with courage – and some help when you need it.

Tip: Compartmentalizing Grief

You can't! Notice that when you grieve, you grieve any and all of your losses at once. When your grief button is pushed, it can explode old and deep feelings of loss that you are not expecting. Stop expecting to control this.

Recognize your triggers… I was once sitting on the end of the bed in a Cuban hotel, sobbing. I needed a certain number of Cuban pesos to pay the tax at the airport to leave Cuba. I knew why I was feeling so sad. This simple task brought me to tears because it was clearly a "David Task". He would have looked after this detail. He would have saved the cash earlier in the week and made sure we had what we needed.

I found the cash. I solved the problem. I allowed myself to cry and be present with my grief. Knowing the source of my upset allowed me to be self-aware and kind to my grieving heart.

Mental Wellness

What is Mental Wellness?

"Mental health is defined as a state of well-being in which every individual realizes his or her own potential, can cope with the normal stresses of life, can work productively and fruitfully, and is able to make a contribution to her or his community.[12]"

This simple definition is a good start to our conversation about mental wellness. I think it helps to outline that we need our mental health, or to be well mentally, to live our lives productively. It also suggests a concept that I believe wholeheartedly – that we all have struggles in life and, most of the time, we have the resilience to handle it.

When we are mentally well, we still feel a range of emotions, from joy and happiness to sadness and loneliness, but the negative ones do not interfere with our ability to live our lives and deal with our issues. When we falter we need to ask for help and we need to deal with our mental wellness issues head on, rather than allow them to become worsened by a lack of attention.

How Mental Wellness Builds Resilience

We can't be resilient unless we are enjoying a relatively high level of mental health. The struggles we face challenge our mental wellness, so we need to keep a careful eye on how we are doing.

Our mental health can be looked at as a continuum. We can find ourselves closer to the healthy end or the end where we need help.

This help can come in many forms, including support from friends and family, professional therapy and support groups, and/or drug therapy. According to the World Health Organization, more than two-thirds of the people identified with a mental health issue do not seek treatment. The help is there, we just don't accept it.

We need to be open to dealing with issues and not allow social bias to stop us from getting help. Pretending you are okay, in order to meet the expectations of others, is always a bad idea because it erodes your resilience. Better to deal with issues as they are than wait until they worsen and you have even less resources left to apply to the problem.

The social stigma around mental illness and mental health is strong. We don't talk about mental illness, and because of that, we make people who are suffering feel isolated and alone. They may well feel that their situation is strange or unusual.

The fact is, mental health issues like schizophrenia, depression, dementia and alcohol dependence, account for 13% of disease globally. That makes mental illness a larger problem globally than heart disease or cancer. [13] With statistics like that, we all know from personal experience that mental health is an issue.

Many of us have dealt with mental illness ourselves, in myriad ways. We all know of loved ones or friends who have suffered, and we have seen first-hand how difficult this can be. The last thing someone with mental health issues needs is to feel that their condition is judged by others as shameful, a sign of weakness, or not to be discussed in polite company. This adds weight to what is already a heavy load.

What follows are descriptions and examples of the most common mental health issues we face in our society: depression and anxiety, postpartum depression, post-traumatic stress injury, and addiction.

Keeping an eye on these mental health issues is critical to building resilience and remaining resilient.

Depression and Anxiety

Depression symptoms range from mild to severe, but it is clear that the rates of depression are steadily increasing. More and more people are being put on antidepressant medications, which are effective for some people and less so for others. The side effects of these drugs can be an issue and can cause people to stop taking medications. Cognitive behavioral therapy can also be effective, but may not be an option for some who might find availability and/or costs to be an issue.

Anxiety symptoms also vary from mild to severe. Feeling anxious is perfectly normal. However, people with Generalized Anxiety Disorder find it hard to control their feelings of worry. Other conditions that involve anxiety include panic disorder, phobias and post-traumatic stress disorder (PTSD).

Anxiety and depression are often experienced at the same time. This type of disorder affects about 1 in 20 people in the UK.[14]

Grace's Story

Our daughter Grace has always been a sweet, happy soul. She is one of the most caring and people-centered individuals I know. And then, all at once, or so it seemed, she became sad and withdrawn. She had gone from always happy, silly and comical to quiet, grumpy and sad.

It was not hard to see the change. It was not even hard to figure out what had happened. She was struggling with the changing relationship of my new partner. This man had arrived in our lives several months earlier, when Grace was almost twelve.

Grace had been the most accepting of George. She took him on as a new plaything. She goofed around with him. They did things together. He taught her to shoot with a bow and arrow and throw knives. She was having a wonderful time with this new man in her life. But he was just a guy. He was Mom's new partner. He was not a father. He did not have anything to do with her loss.

And then, it happened.

Her little sister, Katie, who had not been nearly as accepting of George thus far, suddenly put her hand in his one day, and became his little girl. She had decided that this man had a place in her life as a step-father.

This completely unsettled Grace, who had never considered that George would take on a role that involved parenting. She was not ready for this. It pushed her grief buttons in a way nothing else had. And so, she became sad. So sad.

We did not know what to do.

Over the years, I had used a great therapist to help me through our difficult journey. She had been there for me when I was uncertain. She had been a great help as I tried to support the kids through their difficult times. She had been wonderful. I took Grace to her, and at Grace's insistence, I stayed in the sessions with her. We attended many sessions. The therapist did her best to get Grace to talk about her feelings, and because Grace is a people pleaser, she said whatever she thought the therapist and I wanted to hear.

111

A few months later, the therapist graduated Grace and suggested that with a little time she would learn to accept George and she would be fine. But she wasn't. She was still sad and sometimes angry. When she looks back on this time now, she calls it, "the time when I hated George." She was still struggling.

A friend suggested another therapist. This woman had had some success with a few people we knew. I took Grace, and this time, left her with the therapist. They talked. I don't know what they talked about, but they basically worked through some delayed grief, some complicated feelings about George and I. And also, some strategies for dealing with general teen social stuff.

Within a month or so, we started to see a change in Grace. She started to be less upset and more often happy. Within a couple of months, she was back to normal. We could not believe the difference. She has continued to be her silly, happy self and we celebrate how lucky we are to have her back.

We are so grateful we had the support of two great therapists, who helped Grace work through her issues. We did not assume the problem would just go away. We did not assume it was just teen angst. It seems to me that it is better to be safe than sorry. Better to get help than to suffer through, hoping things will get better.

Consider this: if my child began to have chronic stomach aches, I would take her to the doctor. If that doctor could not help, I would take her to another doctor, and another, until the problem was solved. So, why not take the same approach with my child's mental health?

What a wonderful, life-long lesson we teach our children when we encourage them to seek help when they don't feel mentally healthy. We can do this by getting help for ourselves, too. When Grace went to a therapist, she was used to her mom going, and so it was not a big deal.

In our home, we get help when we need it.

Postpartum Depression

When I was pregnant for the first time, I was not sure what to expect. I read the books. I heard all the advice. I attended classes with other soon-to-be parents. There was one lecture during a pre-natal class that I will never forget.

The instructor, who, up until that point, had been jovial and collegial, became very serious and stern. She said, "Now, I need you to listen well. I need you to know that there will come a day when you will be so tired, so frustrated with your crying newborn, that you will feel like you might hurt the baby. When this happens, I want you to put the baby in the middle of the floor, and leave the room. I want you to shut all the doors you walk through and keep walking until you can't hear the baby crying anymore. Then stay in that place until you feel ready to go back and deal with your baby."

I was shocked. I remember thinking, "Are you serious? Really?"

She then explained about how parents, even the good ones, feel pushed to the limit by the lack of sleep and changes to lifestyle that come with a new baby. They react in unexpected ways, with the result being shaken baby syndrome, or worse. At the time, I thought she was exaggerating. I thought that would never happen to me. Later, I reflected on the moments when I could imagine needing that advice, and how tired and worn out we were at times.

This was really the only thing we learned about managing emotional wellness with a new baby. There was really nothing about postpartum depression (PPD) in that course.

There should have been.

113

That was over twenty years ago and I know that PPD was less talked about then. It is still not commonly understood; and in fact, the situation the instructor described aligns pretty well with what most people think they know about the condition.

When I spoke recently to a friend about PPD, she started talking about a case from way back when a woman drove into a lake with her children in the car. She was reported to be suffering from depression. Another friend said that all he knew about PPD was that it was when women did not love their children and wanted to hurt them. This could not be farther from the truth, in most cases, but it informs why women are afraid to talk about their sadness after childbirth. Who wants to be put in the group of mothers who hate their children?

The problem is, if all you know about this condition are the extremes, you may not be ready to deal with the more common forms, which affect many of us. You may feel, as the new mom or her family, that the whole topic is too scary to talk about. The same stigma that affects mental illness in general stops new moms and their caregivers from wanting to deal with the symptoms when they arise. This is supposed to be "the happiest time of your life" and so you better make sure it's pretty fabulous, or keep up a good façade, at the very least.

There are three types of Postpartum Depression[15]. They are generally referred to as "the baby blues", depression and psychosis.

I have experienced two of them, as have about one in every ten women. Think about that for a minute. You probably can think of several women you know who have experienced childbirth, and yet how many have mentioned PPD? Not many, right? There are a lot of women apparently not talking about their experience, and are, therefore, suffering in silence.

This can't make it easier, and in many cases, it must make the condition worse and more long lasting. That was my experience.

The first type is often referred to as the "baby blues" and are considered normal. Most women experience this – the sudden mood swings, including feeling very happy, and then very sad.

I recall feeling very sad and crying the day after I delivered my first baby. I was still in the hospital. I was confused and concerned about how I was feeling until the nurse came into the room and caught me crying.

Now, I was confused, concerned, and embarrassed. I was having the "happiest time of my life" after all. Right? The nurse sat down beside me on the bed and explained that the baby blues were perfectly normal, they were the result of the extreme swings in hormone levels right after birth. She advised that I not worry about it, but to let my doctor know if they continued more than a couple of weeks. I don't recall feeling them again. Thank goodness for great nurses.

The second, more serious type of PPD, happens when moms feel sadness, despair anxiety or irritability that is more severe than that of "baby blues". This form of depression can happen a few days or even months after childbirth. The symptoms interfere with the woman's ability to do the things she needs to do every day.

In my case, this hit about six months after my second child was born. I was surprised again. I thought I might have baby blues again, but I was not anticipating the sadness and feelings of desperate loneliness I felt after my second baby. There seemed to be no good reason. The baby was perfect. She almost never cried, she was easy to nurse, she slept well, and by the time I started to feel sad, she was already six months old. I remember being left at home with the two kids, my oldest now three and a half, and wondering how I was going to get through the day. I was so sad. I tried to explain this to David, but his response to the statement, "I'm not feeling well and I need you to stay home" was "What's wrong?"

Since I could not answer that question with a list of symptoms, he was confused and suggested, "I'll try to get home as early as I can today." He really did not get it, and I was doing a bad job of explaining it.

This went on for a couple of weeks. I only mentioned it to a couple of people and they were not helpful. One told me that my problem was that David did not do his share of the housework. This was both untrue and not helpful, but it's a great example of someone not knowing what on earth to say to someone who says they feel sad and depressed. As friends and family, we need to get much better at listening and refrain from trying to solve problems we don't understand.

The worst day I can remember from this period was the day that I really wondered if I should be left alone with the kids. I was not concerned that I would harm them. Not at all. I was just concerned that I was not good company and I did not have the energy to cook meals and do the necessary care work. Again, David went to work. Then a girlfriend called and asked if she could drop a couple of kids off for me to watch while she went into town to run a few errands. I wish I had said no. I could not admit how badly I was feeling. She dropped the kids off and I faked it while she was there. I managed through the day but felt even more isolated because I could not talk about my feelings. Again, I did not feel that I was going to harm anyone, including myself, I just felt incredibly sad.

After a few weeks these feelings subsided. Gradually, I began to feel better. I felt more myself. I was fortunate. Many women will suffer much longer and will require medication and counselling. Luckily, we have come a long way in our understanding of how to diagnose and treat this condition – as long as women seek help or someone seeks help for them.

For me, this was a wakeup call to never take my mental health for granted. I am not so strong that I can't be brought down by depression. I have to pay attention. Now, I get help when I need it. I don't wait. I'm grateful for this learning.

The third type of PPD is called **Postpartum Psychosis.** This is a very serious mental illness where women lose touch with reality and may have auditory hallucinations and delusions. They often suffer insomnia and feel agitated and angry. Women suffering from this type of depression need treatment right away, including medication. They may need to be hospitalized. This is the PPD that most people seem to think of when they hear about new moms and depression. It is this condition that drives women to harm themselves and others. It affects one in one thousand women.

While we need to support the women struggling with this affliction, we also need to recognize that this is not the PPD most women encounter. You don't need to have these extreme symptoms to seek help. Every woman who suffers deserves a safe space to talk about how they are feeling and get help.

Joanna's Story

Joanna was a strong farm girl who grew up knowing the value of work. She was educated with a Bachelor of Science degree and had a job in her field. When Joanna and her husband found out they were having twins, they were a little apprehensive, as this was their first pregnancy and not at all what they were expecting. The extra health risks of carrying and delivering healthy twin babies gave Joanna much anxiety and she pored over books and websites dealing with twins and twin pregnancies. She was supported by a great team of doctors and her family, and after a few minor issues, Joanna delivered her twin boys successfully and took them home. All was well.

Joanna's family and friends were supportive of the new family. They came together and created a schedule to make sure dinners were cooked and someone was there daily to help out with the babes.

Joanna was not feeling like the happy new mom she thought she should be. Despite the gift of these two perfect babies, she felt terrible. She recalls sitting at the table, looking at a meal that had been lovingly prepared for her and thinking, "I just can't eat." She also recalls being given the opportunity to lie down, while someone else watched the boys, and lying in bed staring at the ceiling and wondering, "I'm so tired. Why can't I sleep?"

She was nursing the babies successfully, despite feeling more and more emotionally uncomfortable. She was noticing her discomfort and those around her were seeing it, too.

When it came time for the babies' two-month checkup, her mom and husband sent her in to speak to the doctor on her own. The doctor, who had been primed for this conversation, asked Joanna what was going on. The doctor told Joanna that she "looked grey" and suggested that she start to supplement the boys breast milk with some formula. She also suggested a mild anti-depressant that was safe for a breastfeeding mom and her babies.

From that point, Joanna and her husband tried a new regime. Her husband fed the babies late in the evening, which allowed Joanna to sleep for five uninterrupted hours. Joanna took her meds and began to get outside for walks on a regular basis. She started to feel better.

Fast forward five years and Joanna is pregnant again. She has long stopped taking her anti-depressants and now asks her doctor what the chances are that she will feel as bad after her second delivery as she did after her first. The doctor tells her that her likelihood of having postpartum depression again is quite high. She says they will keep a close eye on her.

Good thing.

Joanna delivers a beautiful baby girl and now has five-year-old twins and a newborn to care for. It is winter time in Ontario and she is stuck with these bundles of joy all day on her own. It is dark until eight in the morning and again by five in the afternoon. She is not having a great time and is having a hard time bonding with her new baby. She starts to resent the baby and begins to feel sad again.

But, this time, she knows what is happening and approaches her doctor to have a candid discussion on how much worse her postpartum is this time and her fears of what could happen if she does not get help. She and her doctor find an anti-depressant that works well for her. The sun starts to stay out a little longer and Joanna starts to feel better. Not blissful, but better.

Now, wouldn't it be great if I could share that Joanna is drug free and ridiculously happy now?

But this is real life, and I would describe Joanna more as "strong, brave, self-aware, and ready to share her story so that others can learn from it." Since her daughter's birth, eight years ago, Joanna has struggled with "health anxiety". This is a common condition where people worry and are anxious that they or loved ones are going to get sick, perhaps even die. Joanna worried about not being around to raise her children. She worried about the health of her children and her extended family. When a health crisis that affected her family occurred, she would become so anxious that she would have panic attacks and enter into a worse depression.

119

Because of Joanna's previous experience with looking after her mental health, she got help. With a combination of therapy and medication, Joanna is able to manage her anxiety. It is not gone, but it is managed. As the kids get bigger her worries about not being around for them seems to lessen.

Now, Joanna is reaching out to others around her and sharing her story. She bravely tells others about her suffering and encourages them to talk about any mental health issues they have. She has noticed that sharing her story allows others to open up to her and share their own experiences. She knows this can make a huge difference in the lives of others, while giving additional meaning to her own experience.

Joanna's story also demonstrates the complex process of finding appropriate medications for mental illness. Joanna experienced being prescribed drugs that did not work well, and finding the right drug meant staying on them for a period of time to assess their effectiveness. This process is difficult and frustrating when people are already struggling. Also, what works for one person, may not work for another.

Joanna also noticed that when your mental wellness returns, you are tempted to stop taking the medication that has worked so well. She learned from others that stopping their medication meant they returned to the same depression and anxiety.

This is much like a diabetic, controlling their blood sugar with insulin for several months, and then stopping the insulin. Without the support of their insulin medication, the diabetic's blood sugar will be right back where they started, in a potentially life-threatening situation.

Part of the strong stigma about mental illness seems to support the idea that taking medication keeps you from the ranks of "normal" people, so once you feel okay again, the medication can be stopped.

The goal in mental wellness is to stop the symptoms of illness, so you can function well in your life. If that requires a medication, so be it. We need to take the lead from Joanna and continue to talk about mental health as the medical condition it is. It is a shared experience that is too often treated as though it were shameful and rare.

Post-Traumatic Stress Disorder

The following quote is from the Canadian Department of National Defence video on Post-Traumatic Stress Disorder (PTSD):

> "PTSD is a physical condition in which the chemical signals of the brain change, which can affect a soldier's behaviour in theatre and once back home. While doctors are optimistic that treatment programmes can relieve many of the symptoms, much about the disorder is still unknown, and it can take years for the symptoms of PTSD to be felt and recognized."16

Although the acronym "PTSD" seems to be still commonly used, the term "disorder" is often being changed out for "injury". This is to recognize that PTSD happens as a direct result of the difficult experience the sufferer has endured. This injury is no different than a lost leg or arm, it just happens to be in the head and heart of the person and cannot be easily seen from the outside.

We know that PTSD affects many people, not just soldiers, but the same rules apply. People who develop this injury have difficulty living their lives as the trauma seems to be re-lived in their minds, both while asleep and awake. The condition is known to affect first responders, like police, fire and ambulance, and can affect anyone who is in a traumatic situation.

Lieutenant General Roméo Dallaire

I heard Roméo Dallaire speak in Ottawa at a conference of public service managers. He spoke about leadership. I recall less of what he said about leadership and much more about my awareness that this man had survived the unthinkable and lived to tell the story. Now that his story has been told, many times over and in several books, we know that he suffered immensely from the operational injury of Post Traumatic Stress Disorder (PTSD). He has since become a strong advocate for those who suffer from this injury.

In Dallaire's book, "Waiting for First Light: My Ongoing Battle with PTSD", he talks extensively about the lack of support he received during and after his experience in Rwanda. He talks about how difficult the experience was, and how he tried to forget about it when he got home:

> "Sure, it was a war, but it was still my job, what I was trained for, no big deal. Now let's get back to being a general in Canada. The worst part was that I felt compelled to fall into that, and to minimize what I had gone through, what Rwanda had endured. At work I felt compelled not to talk about my state of mind, my fatigue and sense of disconnection. I was proud, I guess, of my ability to cope—and sometimes nearly guilty for having been away for a year. The implication was that now I was doing work for real people: Canadians. The unspoken corollary: Rwandans

weren't real people. That really ate away at me."17

He felt that there were no supports in place when he got home, no one wanted to hear about the horrors he had seen and experienced.

"Again, this is not an unusual situation. It is difficult for all vets of such catastrophic and complex missions to come home and discover that no one really wants to know what they witnessed, what they did. Maybe at first your spouse will listen to you pour your heart out all night long. But the next time, it's only for an hour or two. By the third time, they are interrupting to ask if you remembered to feed the dog or take out the garbage. You are not supposed to grieve too much, or too long. Too often, your friends and loved ones believe you need to forget the whole thing; and the less they know about it, the more they think they are helping you to get over it."18

"The problem is that you simply can't do it, because it just happened. Just now. Either in flashbacks or in dreams. And so, you try to blot it out by any means: medication and therapy, drugs and alcohol, whatever will throw you off this playing field of horror."19

"Just as I must accept that the Rwandan genocide will never leave me, I now accept that my injury will never heal. For me, treatment came too late. The wound was allowed to fester too long, to infect too deeply. I can see now—as I couldn't while I lived it—that pretty much everything I did, or that was done to me, over those first years after I came home from Rwanda exacerbated my condition... I am an object lesson in how not to treat a returning veteran with PTSD."

General Dallaire makes a strong case for the support that those with PTSD should be receiving. He feels that if we have resources available to repair damaged hearts, kidneys, amputations or eyesight, we should be resourcing PTSD. We need to learn more about this injury, and how to treat it. Treatment will need to be tailored to the needs of the individual, as this is an illness that affects everyone differently.

"Urgent treatment is not only essential to the injured veterans—many of whom still have fifty or sixty years of living ahead of them—but for their families. PTSD can ripple out to harm the people around the primary sufferer: parents, spouses and children all suffer from the consequences of the injury when it results in alcoholism, abuse, neglect or divorce. Evidence is now emerging that the teenaged children of PTSD-injured vets are themselves sometimes committing suicide. It is essential for the injured, their families, their friends and the entire care community to understand what PTSD actually is, and how it uniquely affects today's military veterans. Only when we truly understand the injury and take action to head off and to mitigate its impact will we be able to say that we recognize the real costs of peacekeeping, peacemaking and war."20

I am grateful to General Dallaire for his openness and willingness to share his personal experience for the benefit of others. For so long, this injury has been considered a weakness and has been a source of shame for sufferers. The constant and determined approach this man has taken in sharing his story, and helping us understand this condition, has made it possible for others to come forward to seek and receive treatment. He leaves an important legacy and demonstrates resilience despite his suffering.

Addiction

For those with addiction, thinking about resilience might seem like putting the cart before the horse. In a way, the addict needs the horse to crash through the cart and leave it looking like a pile of sticks, before it can be rebuilt in a way that includes resilience. An addict is in survival mode.

Out of respect for the suffering of these individuals, I reiterate my caution that The Resilience Way is intended as a guide for those with relatively good mental health. I would not expect that the thoughts and ideas in this book would harm anyone, but I want to be clear that those with significant mental health and addiction issues need to find professional help so that they can be properly supported in their journeys.

Nevertheless, I offer this section as information for those with addiction issues and those who love someone with these issues, in the hope that it might be helpful.

For background, and to frame the topic, the definition of addiction is:

"Addiction is the repeated involvement with a substance or activity, despite the substantial harm it now causes, because that involvement was (and may continue to be) pleasurable and/or valuable."

There are four key parts to this definition of addiction:

1. Addiction includes both substances and activities (such as sex and gambling).

2. Addiction leads to substantial harm.

3. Addiction is repeated involvement despite substantial harm.

4. Addiction continues because it was, or is, pleasurable and/or valuable.[21]

David Rosenberg's Story

For David Rosenberg, life had never been easy. He recalls a childhood of feeling "uncomfortable". He never felt that he fit in. He suffered from anxiety and depression and was later diagnosed with bipolar disorder. By the time he got to high school, he was in a world where he felt he did not belong.

Despite his issues, after high school, David followed a path to "success". But this was success based on others' expectations. He went to university, joined the family business, got married and bought a house. He built a family; including three children. It all looked good from the outside. David was a good actor. He was funny and he used his humour to hide the pit in the bottom of his stomach. He was looking for something to take away that constant, uncomfortable feeling.

He found that release in crack cocaine. David tried crack once and discovered that it took away his discomfort. He was immediately hooked. Three years and four hundred thousand dollars later, he had lost his wife, his kids and his house.

So, as I warned, the solution for David is not in The Resilience Way. No amount of personal values, work, nor good diet, and exercise, were going to solve David's problems. He had to hit rock bottom. He needed his entire family to abandon him before he could see that the consequence of using crack was worse than the relief it provided.

According to David, in this moment, the addict sees that he/she is powerless over the drug. In this surrender lies the addict's victory.

David is now a "Sober Coach" and says:

> "When the parent of an addict calls me and asks what they should do, my first question is to ask where the addict is living. Invariably they say he/she is living at home. I tell the parent they need to kick them out of the house. The parent will try to say that they can't do that, for fear that their child will die. I point out that the child will die either way, if we don't get them off the drugs. You need to kick them out so that they can hit their rock bottom and surrender to the drug. Only then can they start the work of recovery."

Recovery involves dealing with the underlying issues that created the addiction in the first place, and then creating a toolbox for dealing with life's problems. This toolbox approach provides the recovering addict with specific ideas about how to handle decision making, relationship issues, and daily challenges. Some examples might be, "If in doubt, don't do it" or "when making big decisions, don't do it alone.'

In David's experience, when you start thinking you don't need the toolbox, you get into trouble. When you start thinking you are able to deal with situations on your own or deal with challenges as others might, you step into dangerous territory. An addict must always recognize their potential to falter and keep the tools that work best close at hand.

And a word about spirituality, from the experience of this Sober Coach...

> "It helps to believe in a higher power, that someone else is driving the bus. The concept of "God" is difficult for me, so I think of that higher power as "The Universe". For my clients, I suggest that it is not critical to believe in a higher power, it is just important that you don't think that you are the higher power. You need to recognize that there are many things that are outside of your control."

In summary, this whole discussion of mental wellness is intended to help us understand and accept that this topic is important and necessary.

The continuum idea, the idea that we are all on a continuum between great mental wellness and serious mental illness, helps me remember that this topic always applies to me.

I have never had perfect mental wellness, and neither have you. Resilient people recognize this and consider their placement on the continuum and what that means to their resilience.

At what point do I need some help? Who can help? Asking questions and being aware is a much better approach to mental wellness than thinking that mental illness is shameful, must be kept a secret, and refusing to admit we are struggling.

Resilience is about getting help for that sore shoulder or knee, or that addiction or depression, before it becomes a much bigger problem.

Spirituality

What is Spirituality?

> "An attempt to seek meaning, purpose and a direction of life in relation to a higher power, universal spirit or God. Spirituality reflects a search for the sacred."
>
> Donald Meichenbaum, University of Waterloo

How Spirituality Builds Resilience

With the broad definition of spirituality in mind, we look for spirituality to enhance our resilience by encouraging:

- Faith-based feelings of gratitude (beyond just feeling grateful to other people)

- Forgiveness based on stronger feelings of empathy and love

- Feelings of love for and being loved by a higher power

- Feelings of "awe" or connection to the larger universe

Not Necessarily Religious

The benefits of spirituality do not stem from our participation in religious activities (like attending church), but from our internal beliefs and values relating to our faith. Our faith provides a clear sense of values that make life worth living and help connect us to the larger universe. The result: Positive emotional feelings that help us through the tough times.

The belief in a higher power can be found throughout history, and in every culture. Evidence for beliefs in an afterlife goes back at least 100,000 years. Every known human culture has creation myths, with the possible exception of the Amazonian Pirahã people, who also lack number words, color words and social hierarchy.[22]

Spirituality and religion are not as common in some parts of the world as in others. The table below shows the differences in three western countries. However, it also points out that in all three cases there are many people who don't participate in organized religion, yet do believe in a higher power.

Country	Participate in Organized Religion	Believe in God or a Higher Power
USA	50%	80%
Canada	21%	67%
UK	36%	55%

Source: See notes 23, 24, 25, 26

Connection to a Higher Power

In the Canadian case, only nineteen percent describe themselves as "pure non-believers." This means that for more than eighty percent of Canadians, their resilience is supported by their spirituality. This is not surprising. Psychologists, philosophers, anthropologists and neuroscientists have long studied human beings natural predisposition to believe or have faith in a higher power.

> Spirituality seems to play an important role in our emotional and social lives.

Rituals are a part of this. Many people who don't participate in religious activities on a regular basis, still show up for holidays, weddings, funerals and other milestones. These occasions connect us to our culture and to our community. They just feel right.

Our spirituality also helps us to feel more grateful. According to research, those higher in religiosity and spirituality are more inclined to experience feelings of gratitude than those who are less religious or spiritual.[27] In my experience, the simple fact that I believe in a higher

131

power makes me notice that not all of my gifts are the result of my actions and efforts. I am grateful to the universe for all that I have been given. I don't take it for granted.

Studies also suggest that in some ways we are becoming more spiritual. According to Pew Research Center, six-in-ten adults now say they regularly feel a deep sense of "spiritual peace and well-being." Half of people surveyed experience a deep sense of "wonder about the universe" at least once a week. This shows a seven-percent increase in both of these measures of spirituality in the last decade.[28]

> "We are not human beings in search of a spiritual experience. We are spiritual beings immersed in a human experience."
>
> Wayne Dyer

When it comes to resilience, I believe that it helps to believe that you are not alone in your struggles. There is comfort in the knowledge that you are connected to the larger universe and that you are supported by the energy of the universe. There is hope in the knowledge that you are not in control of everything that is happening, and that things can get better in ways you might not expect. Many resilient people find strength in their belief in some higher power.

Nicole's Story

In the late spring of 2012, Nicole, a mother of two, and family doctor with a thriving practice, found a small lump in her breast. She did not think much about it and, as is common with physicians, ignored it for a while. After a few weeks, Nicole had another physician look at it, who also said it was probably nothing. By this time, however, Nicole was not so sure and asked for further investigation. The physician/friend suggested a couple of tests.

Four weeks had passed and the lump had grown to the size of a softball, and no longer did anyone think it was probably nothing. An MRI and a core biopsy confirmed the worst.

Nicole received the fax with her results at her office on a Monday morning. It was now a huge tumor growing very, very aggressively and the report did nothing to calm her worst fears.

The next week went like this... pathology Monday, surgeon Tuesday, oncologist Wednesday, chemotherapy Thursday. She found herself unable to fathom how this had happened, and so quickly. Now her reality included telling her two young children about the situation. The kids immediately asked, "Is this going to kill you?" She and her husband had to admit that although that was not their plan, there was a good chance that the cancer would kill her.

When planning her treatment, the doctors had decided to give this 41-year-old mother of two everything they could. They pulled out absolutely everything they had. She got chemo every two weeks instead of every three. She received the highest dosages possible. In the end, the planned eight weeks of chemo stopped at six because the lung damage she had experienced made it impossible to continue.

After the rounds of chemo, Nicole went straight into radical surgery, including a full axillary node dissection, and then six weeks of daily radiation, and a second surgery three weeks later. The treatment nearly killed her, but miraculously it worked. Five years later, she is cancer free.

The amazing part of the story is not just that she survived, but how she survived, and the credit she gives to her faith in allowing her to survive.

Here is how Nicole describes her experience:

"I had two very profound experiences. One was right after we finished chemo and we were in a pretty low spot. In a span of 12 weeks I had lost 35 pounds. I was like skin and bone, I couldn't walk, I could barely eat and they were trying to figure out if I was going to have radiation treatments or not. The radiation oncologist felt very strongly that I needed it. The team of doctors talked to other doctors in Ottawa — they would have "grand rounds" where all the oncologists would get together and try to decide if they could give me radiation or not. They felt I needed it for therapy, but were concerned that they might do more harm than good.

"It's hard for anyone who hasn't gone through this to understand, but that was perhaps the lowest point in my whole treatment. The uncertainty... do we do this? do we not? The outcome was so unclear. I remember saying over and over again: okay God, nobody seems to know, nobody seems to know what we are supposed to do here. I can't make a decision - you are going to have to make this clear because I can't anymore. It doesn't matter what research I do or my husband (also a physician) does, we can no longer lean on our own understanding.

"I kept repeating the scripture:

'Trust in the LORD with all your heart and do not lean on your own understanding.'

"And another passage:

'In all your ways acknowledge Him, and he will make straight your paths.'

"It was like a mantra for me, I just kept saying that scripture over and over, basically saying I can't do this, I am so weak, I don't even care anymore. I'm so tired. It doesn't even matter. I am so weak and so done with it. And we had prayed, and said, Lord give insight to the physicians and give them the path you want us to take because we are trusting you to lead these physicians in charge of us. We are trusting they are going to feel your nudge.

"And we suddenly get this phone call, out of the blue, and it's the radiation oncologist who says: 'We have a spot for you at 8 o'clock tonight for radiation treatment.' But I didn't feel comfortable with that phone call, it left me feeling incredibly anxious ...here we are, three weeks with no information, except the occasional phone call saying we don't know yet, we have to talk with more people, and suddenly, this phone call out of the blue.

"It's late fall, it's pouring rain, pitch black. The kids are home from school - they're pretty young, and we say, "Kids we have to leave now." So, Mark carries me to the car and the whole way there I'm crouched on the passenger side and weeping, because I feel completely insecure about what we are doing. I feel no peace about launching into 6 weeks of treatment that might do more damage than good in terms of trying to beat this.

"And so, we arrive at the cancer center, Mark pulls over, and takes me into the waiting room of the oncology department. I'm in this huge parka and I'm standing in the middle of the waiting room just shaking and crying – I looked like a total nut bar I'm sure. Mark was parking the car, and then I turn around and he is walking into the waiting room with the pastor of our church and his wife. I thought that Mark must have called them on our way, recognizing that were at the end of our rope. So, they came up and Mark said I was going in for radiation, and they said we are going to pray for you right now. We stood there in the waiting room and they prayed for me and I felt intense strength and peace about it. I said to my husband afterward, 'Did you call them?' and he said, 'No I didn't, they weren't here for you.' It turned out that they got called to visit somebody else who was dying in another part of the hospital, and as they tried to return to their car they ended up coming through a different door because of construction. The person upstairs wasn't even a member of our church - it was the brother of a parishioner. They came to the oncology waiting room. The whole way there I had been thinking: 'Lord just send me a sign that I'm supposed to be doing this - send me some comfort that this is actually what you want me to do.' And there they were. I think it was providence, I don't think it was chance.

"I had another experience when I finished my surgery and was flat on my back, unable to move, in unbelievable pain. I had gone straight from surgery to radiation and I was lying in bed. It was the night after I had a double mastectomy. I was at home but was unable to roll myself over, trapped in bed. My husband was not sleeping in the same bed with me at that point, because I was in so much pain. He was sleeping in the guest bedroom and checking on me periodically. I had gone to sleep that night and had a terrible dream, that everything awful that I thought could happen to me, happened. Everything I had gone through was for nothing - it was just an awful dream. I woke up with an incredible panic attack - only the second one I have had ever in my life. The first one was right around the time they told me I was sick. The panic attack started around two o'clock in the morning and it went on for hours - I couldn't even call out for Mark to come. So, I was lying in bed for hours on end, sweating, with this impending sense of doom. I usually would find comfort by reciting scripture. I kept trying to recite some scripture to myself but I couldn't. I couldn't come up with the scripture, I couldn't.

"So after about an hour and a half, I thought, okay I'm just going to visualize comfort. I'm not normally a visualization person, I'm not someone who visualizes God or Jesus - that's just not how my brain works. The only thing I could come up with was a picture of Jesus, an image of him sitting there on my bed, comforting me, telling me everything was going to be okay. So, all I had was this image. Thank goodness, that actually worked for me - it took about an hour but I was able to calm down.

"Mark came in around 7 o'clock in the morning, gets me set up in bed for the day and he goes off to work. I was able to get my laptop set up and at 8:00 in the morning an email comes in from someone who I had seen twice in my life, someone I barely even knew, a Christian from another church who had obviously been praying for me. She said: 'I woke up very early this morning, praying for you, feeling like you were being attacked and I wanted you to know that as I was praying I had this vision that Jesus is sitting right beside you on the bed, he is right there and wants to remind you that you are going to be okay. You're going to be okay and you are fine just the way you are. You don't have to worry about anything, because it will all be okay."

She went on to explain, "I woke up at 4 o'clock, in a panic and all I could think about was you and as I was praying for you I had this clear picture that you were being attacked, that you were in a black and bleak position and that you needed comfort. Jesus was right there next to you.

"Now, this is someone I met twice in my life; someone I had no relationship with whatsoever. So, there is connection. We are all connected, you can call it spirituality, you can call it whatever you want, there is an inter-connectedness. We all care for each other and are prompted to provide care and connection to those who are suffering.

"I believe if you are connected to that spirituality, if you actually stop and attend to it, act on it, amazing things will open up in your life. You can call it whatever you want. In my life it's Jesus, it's the Holy Spirit, it's God. But for other people it may be something else. It's all the same."

Nicole wonders if people who hear her story will think it's crazy to think that these events were anything more than coincidence. Not that she cares. For her, it's clear that this is "providence" and that her spirituality was a key part of her survival during some desperate moments, and in the day-to-day struggle of a difficult cancer journey.

Death

In Nicole's story, her spirituality provided significant support. It is also clear that she looked to God to clarify the path for her. She did not know whether she would live or die, but she was ready for either. She trusted in God to create the path for her, whatever that might be. In this way, Nicole confronted death, with the comfort of knowing she was not alone, no matter what happened.

This comfort is available to all of us, no matter our specific beliefs, if we are open to the support of a higher power. This is how we become resilient with respect to death.

Fear of death makes it impossible to live a truly resilient life.

I no longer fear death. I have watched David come to terms with death and I watched him die. I have this conversation about death in the Spirituality section because, for me, my comfort with death stems from my belief that there is a higher power; and that there is more to this universe than the life we are living right now. That allows me to feel curious and more comfortable with death.

Our fear of death is mainly a Western phenomenon. If you look at other cultures, including the East Asian philosophy of death, you will not find this fear, but rather death is used as a reminder to enjoy life.

According to The Dalai Lama:

> "The advantage of developing an awareness of death is that it will help you make your life meaningful. You will regard the enduring peace and happiness as more important than short-term pleasure."29

In other cultures, people talk about death. In the West, we try to ignore it, as if we can stop it from happening by not talking or thinking about it. But this clearly does not work.

Headlines everywhere tell us about the newest and greatest "death avoiding" options. We end up behaving in ways that are purely emotional, rather than rational. We force ourselves to eat foods we hate; we pay a fortune for vitamins and supplements; we obsess about exercise; we head to the doctor when we feel anything out of the norm – all in fear of death.

Our culture supports these behaviors because they are a normal part of "a healthy lifestyle". But is our obsession with being healthy making us unhealthy? Some of us are ending up with mental health issues, like health anxiety, as a result of our fear of death.

A survey from 2014 showed that eight in ten adults in the UK are uncomfortable talking about death, and only a third have written a will.[30] So instead of dealing rationally with death, the ultimate conclusion to our time here on earth, we spend our time and energy (both precious resources) burying our heads in the sand.

I am not suggesting that you should not take care of your health. You should. You should do it because, although you will most certainly die, many of us are going to live for a long time, and if we want to enjoy our later years, we need to keep our bodies as able as possible. You should be focused on exercising in order to delay the day when you can no longer walk, breathe comfortably and generally remain active.

The truth about death, in Western culture, is reserved for the chosen few. Or so it seems.

If you talk to someone who has lost a loved one and cared for that person in their dying days, or if you have come to terms with your own mortality, you are probably not as afraid of death as the rest of the people you know. Those who face their imminent death, as David did, learn not to fear it. They learn to focus on the positive and on accepting that death will come.

David used his usual, humorous approach when getting closer to his death. When someone would ask: "How are you?", he would respond with: "I don't think today is the day." I know it took people aback at first, but honestly, what a great way to think about life. Even in those days when we knew time was short, this simple statement made me focus on enjoying that day, that moment. He was so right. That was not the day.

If you wake up in the morning and you feel more or less like you did yesterday, you will probably make it through the day. So, let's focus on enjoying this day. Who knows what tomorrow will bring?

People who know they are dying tend to focus on what makes life meaningful. As my friend Andrea has said, "Time and energy become a currency, not to be wasted."

The day David died was not like those days when he said "Today is not the day." In his final hours he was not fully conscious, and we had him well drugged to keep him comfortable. It was "the day", but he was not suffering.

This brings me to another fallacy, or unfounded worry, that people tend to have. Most people fear death, partly because they think it will be fraught with pain, discomfort and suffering. The majority of us will die in a slow, gradual way, and we will have health care professionals around us who can make sure we are not uncomfortable.

When David died, there was no pain. He spent a day and a half going in and out of consciousness. His sister, Rhonda, had arrived about a half-day before he lost his ability to speak and they had some time together. When he was conscious, we talked to him and he understood us. We sang songs to him and he wiggled his toes. My friend told him she would look after us and he gave her "the thumbs up". People said their goodbyes. Eventually, the nurse who was with us in our home, told me I should tell him that he could go, that he could move on from this world. I did. He died surrounded by his dearest loved ones. It was peaceful.

There is a reason the nurse knew that "it was time". She knew because she helps families through these moments over and over again, and they are more similar than they are different. She knew because the dying have a process. They get to a point when they are ready to move on. This is not something to fear.

We need to realize, of course, that not all deaths happen like this. Some death is traumatic. In some situations, we have no warning. In some situations, there is pain. We don't get to control this. We just have to deal with the reality of our lives, and deaths. I'm certain, however, that spending your life trying to avoid traumatic death is a certain way to not live a full life at all.

Where We Go

From my personal experience, I know that death is not something to fear because it is not the end game. For me, knowing there is something, some experience or state of being beyond this world makes it easier for me to remain rational about death.

In my mind, this idea links to resilience because our lack of comfort with death stops us from making reasonable plans for the future. People don't plan for illness, they don't put money away for retirement, they don't prepare for the fact that they will not always be here. I think many are unable to do these things because they are not comfortable with their beliefs about what happens after death.

I believe that within spirituality there is space to come to terms with or define our thoughts about death and what comes next. If you actually think that when you die you are buried and that's it, of course you are fearful. That's a pretty dismal outlook. And it's a different outlook than most of the world.

The concept that the energy of our lost loved ones does not leave us is not new, and it is a belief common to many religions. Since the beginning of time, people have believed that there is more to death than we can see. The majority of the world's religions believe in some kind of existence after death. Is it really even possible that there is nothing? I don't believe so.

My beliefs are built not on a religious background, but on my experience. My Christian teachings certainly opened my mind to the possibilities beyond death, but the specific ideas of heaven, hell, or resurrection into paradise on earth left me uncertain as to how it all worked.

Then, while sharing dinner with a few friends, the most profound idea was offered.

The idea was that our soul energy remains in the universe and is available to those who seek it. Now, I am defining "soul energy" as that energy that most certainly exists in our bodies while we are alive, and is gone from our bodies when we die. If you have ever watched someone pass, you know that this happens. Or at least you know that the body remains and the person is gone.

Have you noticed where that energy goes?

I have.

Upon death, the soul energy remains. It is ever present. You need only look for it and it is there.

For me this has happened a few times, with people to whom I had a significant connection. And I don't think this makes me special, to be able to feel this energy. Not at all. I think anyone can feel it if they believe it to be possible.

After David passed, he was constantly with me. His energy was present and I could feel it very strongly. After many months passed, I began to notice that it was not always there. But then when I looked for it, simply by opening myself to its presence, it returned. Perhaps it was still there all the time, but I was just not as acutely aware. I'm not sure. I do know that this energy was an enormous source of strength. I never felt alone.

Connecting to a Spiritual Community

For Nicole, her spiritual community has been a critical part of her journey. She has enjoyed the love expressed by her congregation in the form of time, food, love and prayers.

Several months before David was diagnosed, we began attending our local United Church. In this congregation, we found a group of people who immediately welcomed us and offered their friendship. When David became ill, they supported our family with their love, friendship and hot meals. We are very fortunate to have their support.

I asked Nicole her thoughts about how others, who don't already have the benefits of spirituality in their lives, could begin to discover their spirituality.

She had a simple, yet brilliant idea.

She suggests that anyone can simply reach out to people, or a group of people, who do include spirituality as part of their lives. Find a community or a group of people who share a set of beliefs that resonate with you. Hang out with them. Listen to what they have to say. Be open to their thoughts and ideas. Let them share their knowledge and understanding with you. Eventually, one of two things will happen... either your own spirituality will grow or you will realize that you have not found the right place for your particular brand of spirituality. If the latter is the case, find another spiritual option and try again. Even in this process you will find support and learning that will build your resilience.

EMOTIONAL WELL-BEING

Self-Awareness · Mental Wellness · Spirituality

In this chapter we talked about:

Self-Awareness

The Self-Awareness Continuum – some people are strongly self-aware and others are not at all – Where are you?

Mindfulness – you need to be centered so you can become more aware of your feelings

Knowing Thyself – your personality will drive how you prefer to behave and how you will interact with others

Happiness – you need the long-lasting type of happiness and you can create it for yourself

Gratitude - being grateful is a wonderful way to increase your happiness

Guilt – keep this from getting in your way by dealing with feelings of guilt

Grieving – this is complicated stuff but trust yourself to know what's right for you

Mental Wellness

Depression and Anxiety – watch for signs of sadness and worry, and get help early to deal with them

Postpartum Depression – don't be one of the silent sufferers

Post-traumatic Stress Disorder – early intervention is key

Addiction – don't try to fix this on your own

Spirituality

Spirituality is not Religion – we are becoming less religious and more spiritual

Connection to a Higher Power – helps us to not feel alone

Death – is not as frightening as we think it is

Where We Go – the energy that is our soul remains

Connection to a Spiritual Community – find your people, whoever they are

For more information please visit:
www.theresilienceway.com

Chapter Six

Supportive
Relationships

SUPPORTIVE RELATIONSHIPS

Seek Support · Support Others · Boundaries

The second Element of Resilience we will explore is **Supportive Relationships.**

Human beings were never intended to live independently of one another. Some of our deepest needs are connection and acceptance by others. We need to create relationships that support our journey through life.

The Element of **Supportive Relationships** involves three Factors: **Seek Support, Offer Support** and **Boundaries.**

Resilient people know how to **Seek Support** and in so doing they create strong relationships that help them through the tough times. Those tough times, in fact, serve to build those relationships as the shared support experience deepens the connections between people. Once you survive that tough time, those who were there for you are now proven and trusted supports.

Support Others can be a great strength and is a key part of our resilience. Resilient people understand that they are needed and can be useful to others, so they build strong relationships that allow support to go both ways. By **Supporting Others**, we can build trust and a comradery that allows us to rely on those we have helped when we need them. Support and resilience go hand-in-hand in creating ready resources we can seek out in difficult times.

Boundaries are key in ensuring our relationships are not reducing our resilience, by protecting us from people in our lives who are difficult, destructive, or even abusive. This

149

may involve changing how we react to these people and what they do. If this preventative action doesn't result in sufficient **Boundaries**, you may need to change or end the relationship you have with this person. Our goal is to build relationships that make us stronger and more resilient, so we can be confident of managing difficulties and striving for our goals.

Seek Support

What Does it Mean to Seek Support?

The definition of support is:

> "to hold something firmly or carry its weight, especially from below to stop it from falling."

> Cambridge Dictionary

Seeking support means we have accepted that we don't have all the answers, that we don't even have all the questions! We realize we need help and can't figure everything out on our own. When we are going through difficult times, we need to rely on others to hold us up. If we do not have healthy relationships in our lives, we feel lonely and isolated. We are intended to live in a community and need the support of others, which is not weakness, but rather is healthy and normal.[31]

We should:

- Accept help from others and realize the benefits of asking for help.

- Recognize that people want to do something to help when you're struggling … so, let them.

- Listen to other people, as their insights may help you see your situation differently. The exchange will help you to think things through, whether or not their thoughts are helpful to you or your situation.

- Embrace and use the strength that comes from feeling that you are not alone.

How Seeking Support Builds Resilience

As we build our network of people who support us, we are preparing our foundation for future resilience. When we know *how* to ask for help, we can find the support we need. Very often, the resources we need to solve a problem are present in other people. We just need to ask! Most people are happy to offer help and grateful to have been asked.

We become more resilient and more comfortable and confident in handling our challenges when we know we have the right support people in our corner.

I was lucky enough to grow up with lots of people who supported me. My mom, for instance, did everything in her power to support me. No matter what I wanted to do, she would support me. She was always there for me. In doing this, she also taught me that it's okay to ask for help and to let other people help you.

Over the years I sought support many times. I operated under the assumption that if I had a problem, there was someone around who could help. As I dealt with David's illness and death, I had a huge amount of support from family and friends. Even my business clients supported me through this difficult time.

Thanksgiving Love

David died less than a week before Canadian Thanksgiving.

For David, Thanksgiving was great, because he was guaranteed to be served a few of his favorite things: turkey, mashed potatoes and pecan pie. He missed this holiday in 2012, the year he died. Thanksgiving still happened that year though, first for David, and then for the rest of us, because of the loving gestures of our friends.

The first friendly intervention happened on the Sunday before David died. Our friend Darlene and her daughter Stephanie had let us know that they were bringing us dinner.

Now, you have to realize that there was no reason to believe that David was so close to death. He had been at a baseball game on Saturday, after all. So, when Darlene and Stephanie arrived with a fully cooked turkey and all the fixings for Thanksgiving dinner, David was thrilled and sat with his family at the table to enjoy the meal.

It was an amazing gift, especially as it was really the last full meal he was able to eat. On Monday, he ate a little. On Tuesday, he ate a cupcake for breakfast; the last thing he ever ate. Darlene and Stephanie had given a dying man his final pecan pie, and for a man so fond of his food, it was truly an extraordinary gift.

152

The second Thanksgiving gift came a week later, when our dear friends filled our dining room table with the food and love that we needed. Again, we enjoyed a lovely meal. Again, it was made possible by the caring of others, making it possible for us to get through our first holiday without David.

At the end of the meal, the lovely lady who had cooked the turkey thanked me for having her over for dinner! Funny. But these loving friends had supported us through our first holiday without David and, for those who have experienced loss, these milestones can be especially difficult. They made it bearable.

What Keeps Us from Asking for Help

In my experience, many of us think that asking for help:

1. Is a sign of weakness, or a lack of expertise.

2. Exposes a problem – we can't do everything on our own.

3. Is backwards – we want to help others, but not to accept the return of the favor.

4. Is useless; as we don't have people in our lives who can help us with our problems.

We need to realize that none of these points are correct. We need to become more comfortable with asking for help. Without doing this simple thing, we will struggle to be resilient.

Why We Should Ask for Help

Don't forget that other people want to help you. When we see others struggling from the loss of a loved one, an illness or some other difficulty, we want to do something to help. We don't always know what to do though. So, we bake, send notes and messages, or visit.

As the person in need, it is far better to tell others exactly what will help us. This will allow others to know they can help in a way that truly makes a positive difference.

When you ask someone to complete various tasks that seem overwhelming to you at the time or simply stopping by for tea and listening as you unpack a problem, you gift them with the opportunity to help in a meaningful way. Help others out by asking for help.

When David and I started farming, we had to call in a few acquaintances to learn how to run our cash crop farm. We built friendships through this process that have endured. These individuals were an amazing support when David was sick and after he passed.

David died just as our soybeans needed to be harvested and our winter wheat crop needed to be planted. Our friend Richard dropped by a week or so before David died and told us not to worry about the cropping, he would take care of everything. And he did.

The following spring, I began farming on my own. Richard and another friend, Glenn, were an enormous help. I had to learn how to run the machinery and work up the fields. When I ran the tractor out of fuel in the middle of a field, another friend helped me to figure out how to "bleed the lines" and get back up and running. The support of these friends was such a gift. Without them, moving on would have been an even more difficult situation, and farming on my own would have been nearly impossible.

How to Ask for Help

You may be fiercely independent and, traditionally, not have asked for help. Or maybe you were raised in an environment where asking for help was just not the norm. Perhaps you didn't have supportive people in your surroundings, or that support came at a cost.

For whatever reason, you – and many of us – have not learned to ask for help.

Fortunately, asking for help is not all that difficult, especially if you keep in mind that people *want* to help.

So, to ask for help you need to:

1. **Be specific about what you need.** For example: "Would you please come with me to my next appointment, so you can hear what the doctor is saying and help me make decisions afterwards?"

2. **Ask someone for something they can make happen.** If you need an expert in something you are struggling with and know someone with that knowledge, ask for their help. They will appreciate your trust in them and that you asked.

3. **Share your appreciation.** Make sure you thank people when they help you. If you do, they will be much more likely to want to help next time, as they will know that their efforts made a difference.

Supporting Someone Back to Health

A lovely young woman shared her story of resilience with me. I have known her since she started kindergarten with one of my girls. She has always been a smart, energetic, joyous kid.

When she was thirteen, her family and friends realized that she was becoming dangerously thin. She had begun a regime of "healthy" eating where she only allowed herself fruits and vegetables and stopped eating any foods that contained fat, or other things she considered "unhealthy".

This attempt to eat a healthier diet involved no, or very few, calories. She was wasting away. But she was eating! Everyone saw her eating. No one was concerned or noticed that she was changing her eating patterns. She would prepare a whole meal for her family, and then just eat the parts without calories. Her friends also saw her eating and just noticed that she was the healthiest eater in the pack. But she had begun to control every calorie that she ate and was about to become very ill.

I recall talking to her mom after they had sought help. She felt she had tried to teach her kids about healthy eating, but that somehow it had backfired. However, from the psychology of eating disorders she learned that the problems were not about trying to eat healthy at all. This poor soul was sick.

Now, she is a vibrant, amazing teen, who has the world at her fingertips. She is healthy and perfect. She brings me joy just with her energy. When she talks about the time "when I was sick", she relates that she could not have found healing alone. She has a loving, highly functional family and she credits their support for getting her through her difficulty.

She recognizes now that when she was sick, she spent too much time alone. She was afraid that spending time with friends would expose her to unhealthy eating; and so, she chose to stay home. Now she can see that this made things worse.

Looking back, she also sees her doctors and her therapist as supportive relationships that were critical to her recovery. She credits the help of a specialist who was "very strict". This doctor took control of the situation by limiting her activities unless she put on weight. She was not allowed to attend dance classes or even participate in gym class unless she put on weight. She went to weekly appointments and had to show that she was gaining weight in order to win back these privileges. This was no joke. This kid was under super supervision. Her life was at stake if she did not get well.

And so, she began to gain weight. She worked with a therapist and they talked a lot about control. She says, "I needed to be in control of things, so I controlled my food." She learned some strategies that helped.

Now she says, "What helps now is that I think 'It's not worth it.' As I got better, I could see that it's not worth going back. And now I feel like I can talk to others who are struggling. It helps me when I realize that I have a story I can share that can help others. Now I am more aware that although I should try hard at school and other things, I also know that you only live once. I try not to be so uptight about some things."

The supportive relationships of her family, friends and medical professionals made the difference for this lovely young woman, becoming her supporters at a time when she needed help. Now she sees the opportunity to help others, based on her experience and learning.

That's resilient.

That's becoming stronger from your tough time and finding ways to make sense of it. This teen has been tested since her recovery and demonstrated that she can handle tough stuff and remain strong. Her learning as a very young woman will serve her well as she continues in life. She is well prepared with the resilience she needs to achieve whatever she decides to do next.

We can all benefit from accepting help from those around us. We can also improve our resilience by looking for ways to help other people, as we will learn about in the next section.

Support Others

What "Support Others" Means

When we help other people, we build our resilience.

It helps us when we reach out to others and offer what we can. This might be a listening ear, a warm meal, or help with household chores. You might be offering support to someone close to you, like a family member, or someone you hardly know. In all cases, your help makes a difference to both the giver (you) and the receiver.

Look for ways to **Support Others** using your current talents, as well as stretching your abilities so you are also learning. If you think you are not a good listener, for instance, read a little about good listening skills, and then offer to be a sounding board for a friend who needs that support.

And don't forget that when you are struggling, there may be others in the situation with you. As you support them, you build your own resilience.

In my case, having four children to raise gave me plenty of opportunities to learn about the benefits of supporting others. They were a constant reminder that I was not alone in my struggle.

How Supporting Others Builds Resilience

According to The Dalai Lama:

"The more we care for the happiness of others, the greater our own sense of well-being becomes. Cultivating a close, warm-hearted feeling for others automatically puts the mind at ease. This helps remove whatever fears or insecurities we may have and gives us the strength to cope with any obstacles we encounter. It is the ultimate source for success in life."32

It may seem counterintuitive to think about helping others at a time when you are struggling, but you will find that this brings many benefits to your personal resilience, including:

- Realizing that you are often not the only one suffering (due to the same issue or other issues)

- Positive feelings that come from helping others

- Building solid relationships so that you can call on others when you need them.

My friend Dan recently shared a story with me that contains a great example of someone who exemplified this factor of resilience. His brother John had passed away a few months earlier. John had been a rock in the family, always there to help when you needed help. There were many examples of him lending a helping hand within the family.

The surprising thing was that, at his funeral, many people who knew him had similar stories about how he had helped them. It turned out that, without needing to tell anyone else about it, he spent countless hours and days lending a hand to anyone who needed it. His family was not aware of the number of people who had benefited from John's support. Quietly and without any expectation of a favor returned; he was constantly helping others. It gave purpose to his life; it grounded him; it connected him to others.

It made him more resilient.

David's ability to connect to people, and to gratefully accept their help and support, played a part in his resilience. The family doctor and the surgeon in the small town where we live knew him well. They made house calls and were wonderfully supportive. The chemotherapy nurses spent a day with him every two weeks. It was not long before he was advising them on all things from parenting to finances, and teasing them, too. He brought them coffee and was at the door of the chemo clinic when they arrived in the morning. He took his two chemo nurses and his family doctor out for dinner at one point. He wanted to thank them for all they had done for him. David enjoyed making his oncologist laugh. He saw this man every few months and was fairly certain he did not laugh enough. He made it his personal goal to get him to giggle. It worked; and David was very pleased with himself.

David always openly offered his friendship, advice and sense of humor. In return, he received friendship and support, and felt like a colleague, instead of a victim or even a patient. It was as if they were just all working together on a project.

Sandra's Story (Part Two)

My Aunt Sandra is an amazingly resilient person. Part of her resilience comes from her constant focus on helping other people. Her entire focus when you are with her is on you. Her selflessness is astonishing.

When you start a conversation and she says, 'How are you?', the natural thing to do is answer, and then return the question, 'And how are you?' She completely ignores this question though, and moves on to the next part of the conversation. She does this deliberately so that she does not have to spend her time explaining the status of her health and her current pains and ills. She just does not want to go there.

Sandra was diagnosed with stage four lung cancer a long time ago. Even at the time of diagnosis she was told that surgery was not an option. She has undergone several rounds of chemo, some of which made her terribly ill, and has been told more than once that nothing more could be done. Oh, and by the way, she has never smoked a cigarette in her life!

One of the keys to Sandra's resilience is in her focus on others. She is one of those rare birds who spends all of her time thinking about what other people need. If you visit her, she finds all of your favorite foods in her pantry. She has them there just in case you drop by. If she knows you are coming, she will make the foods you love. She is an amazing cook, a skill she honed in order to make others happy.

When you talk to Sandra, the conversation is usually about you. It is hard to talk about her, as she will move the conversation back to you. Until very recently, she routinely cooked enormous meals for a gang of folks. She is one of the last people I know who sends letters in the mail. When she sees something in the newspaper that she thinks you

161

might like to know about, she cuts it out and sends it to you. And she is never shy with telling you she loves you. She just puts it out there.

Sandra has new friends and old friends. According to her:

> "It's all about the people. When you go to the grocery store you should smile at people and talk to people. That's how you make a new friend. You never know who you will meet."

It's really the opposite of "Stranger Training", where we teach our children to be fearful of those they don't know. We don't build resilience by assuming everyone else in our midst is a potential danger. Sandra makes them all her friends; and before long she will be making them their favorite cookies.

Another powerful way we can support others is by sharing our stories of resilience with one another. By doing so, we help to support others who may have had similar experiences. We show them that they are not alone. And in the process, we find that the sharing of the story is helpful to us, too. We find that in the telling of our stories, we begin to understand our experience in new and deeper ways.

If we take a page from Sandra's book, we will find resilience in helping other people. Even when we are suffering ourselves, we look for opportunities to support those around us. We assume that lending a hand, with no expectation of a payback, will be good for our own situation.

Another great example of accepting the help of a friend happened in David's final hours. We had been at his bedside, with him going in and out of consciousness for a day and a half. When he seemed conscious, we would talk to him. Mostly, we would tell him we loved him.

At one point, he raised his gaze from my face to the face of my dear friend Yvette, who had been with us throughout the entire ordeal. When he caught her eyes, she said, "Don't worry, buddy, I've got them." He gave her a "thumbs up". This man, who had not been able to move more than a toe for over a day, raised his arm and lifted his thumb up. Yvette repeated her promise one more time and again she got the same signal.

In his dying moments, he was accepting the help he needed. He was expressing his gratitude toward a dear friend who has always been a strong helping hand. He died only a couple of hours after receiving Yvette's promise. A promise well kept, by the way.

My friend Darlene gets to know, forevermore, that she cooked the last meal that was enjoyed by David with his family. My thanksgiving guests, who cooked the meal and brought it to us, know that they made our first holiday without David bearable.

Sandra knows she has left a legacy of helping throughout her life. People smile when they see her, because her attitude toward both those she knows and those she does not yet know is one of openness and friendship.

> She clearly builds her own resilience by offering support to others.

Now that we have talked about how our relationships support our resilience, we need to turn our attention to the situations where this is not the case. In the next section we will discuss how at times we need boundaries around the people and relationships in our lives.

Boundaries

Some of the relationships in your life may be reducing your resilience. This can happen for many reasons, but we need to be aware if certain individuals are interfering with our happiness and do something about it.

We need to create **Boundaries.**

Here's what to do:

1. Notice the relationships that are a struggle. You know these relationships because they make you feel uncomfortable, exhausted, frustrated or they fly in the face of your values.

2. Place boundaries around the relationship (if possible).

3. Place boundaries around the individual, if necessary.

Grudges and Forgiveness

One of the important ways we can manage how others are influencing our resilience is by offering forgiveness to those who have wronged us.

When we feel victimized in some way by another person, the answer is not always in cutting off ties and ending your relationship with that person. The problem with this strategy is that although you may be protecting yourself from future harm, you have not dealt with the existing upset.

This is the stuff of "grudges".

Some of us are better than others at holding grudges. I am very competent, for instance, at remembering things that people did to me decades ago. I hold these memories like badges of honor, as if they are evidence of the harm. The problem with grudges though, is that the other person may not even know that you hold this grudge. They may not even recall the incident or be aware that it happened. So, the grudge only hurts the grudge-holder and does nothing to right the wrong.

Grudges eat away at our resilience as they encourage us to focus on the past and on negative aspects of our journey. "Today I decided to forgive you. Not because you apologized or because you acknowledged the pain you caused me, but because my soul deserves peace."

Najwa Zeblan

The key to not holding grudges, and to not allowing past issues with people to interfere with your resilience, is forgiveness. We need to forgive people for the things they do. We need to let go of our upset and move forward with a sense of peace.

Now, if you are thinking that the wrongs done to you are too big for this to be possible, consider the story of Freda.

Freda's Story

Freda grew up in a small town in Ontario. She was a farm girl, a beautiful young woman. One day while she was walking home from school a group of teenage boys lured her into a park and raped her. She told no one. She returned to the high school where she and the boys attended only to find that she now had a reputation for being "easy". Much of her life after this incident was influenced by her feelings of self-doubt and self-loathing. She consistently sabotaged her relationships because she felt unworthy. She even felt that God had abandoned her.

Over thirty years later, having done considerable work on her emotional health, Freda went back to the instigator of her rape and forgave him. Of course, he was shocked. He wondered why she would do this, given the harm he had caused.

She felt that this forgiveness gave her a sense of peace. It allowed her to move forward.

She felt:

"Now I can become the person I'm supposed to be."

This is a strong example of how one woman overcame a horrific experience, partly by forgiving those who caused her harm.

Freda also talks about the power of forgiveness from another angle, that of asking for forgiveness from those you may have wronged.

In her case, she asked her ex-husband for forgiveness for not sharing her story with him and for not being able, during the time of their marriage, to be fully present. Again, she found this experience gave her peace and allowed her to look toward her future. She says that this experience, "opened my spirit... and I became more grateful, able to look forward and focus on my blessings.[33]"

I believe we have important lessons to learn from this woman, who had every right to live out her life in the role of the victim.

Instead, she chose to build her resilience by defining how she would interpret the experiences of the past, and the people involved. She created the **boundaries** around how she now relates to these people.

It's not just about whether you allow people in your life, but how you choose to define your relationship to people who are no longer present, yet have the potential to impact you by virtue of their past involvement. By forgiving, we create space for ourselves.

> "As I walked out the door toward the gate that would lead to my freedom, I knew if I didn't leave my bitterness and hatred behind, I'd still be in prison."
>
> Nelson Mandela

Relationship Awareness

You may well find that there are some people and/or relationships that need to be redefined or changed in some way in order for you to move forward in a healthy way. It may be that you need to change how you relate to someone. It may be that you need to not have this person in your life. You need to figure out what works.

If you think about it, we do this all the time. The relationship you have with your parents when you are ten is not the same as the relationship you have with them when you are forty, or at least it should not be the same. Over time, our relationships change in ways that fit the situation. We get into trouble when either relationships don't change, or we establish new relationships that turn out to interfere with our resilience.

It's not hard to know there is a problem with a relationship, because it feels terrible. If you feel uncomfortable when you are with someone, think about why that is. What is happening?

> What is the person doing that is making you uncomfortable?

Remember, you are responsible for your feelings, so only you can determine why this person's behavior is upsetting you.

Is there an issue with how you or the other person has changed, but the relationship has not changed? Is it that your own development has not been recognized, like a parent who is still treating their forty-year-old like a child? Is there a significant alignment gap in values between you and the other person, so that expectations of behavior clash as you operate under your values, and they under theirs?

You need to spend some time thinking this through so you can determine and design a better way of interacting with this person.

Here is a quick example of a values gap that happens to me whenever I try to interact with people who hold different values than my own.

These are commonly people who spend their time and money making sure that they look good for other people. They have houses, cars, fashion and beauty that are focused on their need to "keep up with the Jones."

This makes no sense to me.

I find myself constantly expecting that someone with these values will behave according to my expectations; perhaps by volunteering their time to help others or having an authentic conversation about themselves.

I find it incredibly frustrating when they can't. But I need to recognize that they are living authentically to their *own* values, which happen to revolve around achievement and status-seeking.

I don't need to approve of these values, but I need to stop expecting a change, because it probably will not happen. By not having realistic expectations of what I can change, I create suffering for myself. Understanding this is critical to my being able to work toward a relationship that is sustainable. The sooner I change my expectations, and the relationship I have with this person, the sooner I can regain the energy I lose trying to make it work. I need to find a way of relating to this person (or not) that does not zap my resilience.

Redefining Relationships

Once you have a clear understanding of where the problem in the relationship resides, you are ready to fix the problem.

Now, let's be super clear... you are not trying to fix the person, only your relationship with them.

In many cases, you are just changing your own reactions to the other person's behavior.

It might be that when that judgmental person speaks, you now say silently, "I choose not to allow that judgment to bother me. I'm happy in my own skin."

It might be that you are no longer going to hold conversations you know are not helpful, and you are going to say, "I'd rather not discuss this, thank you."

In other situations, you may decide that in order to have a constructive conversation with a person, you need to set new ground rules about how you are going to interact. These are courageous conversations and are not easy but can be very important. If you are fearful of how these conversations will go you should keep in mind that most people want to have the best possible relationship with you. They may also know that something is amiss, but they probably don't know what it is... because you have not told them. It's like the employee who gets fired for something their manager never bothered to mention until the day of the firing. Shame on that manager! She should have given the employee feedback much sooner. The same applies to our personal relationships. We owe people feedback when we need things to change. They should have the opportunity to be the support you need them to be.

Perhaps you need, for example, to establish a new way of interacting with a parent. They may be acting in the only way they know how, and a good conversation will help to come to a new understanding of what you need.

Finally, there may be some people who need to exit your life. Those people who bring you suffering, and the relationship cannot be altered, need to stop being in your life. It's just that simple. Whether a family member or friend or acquaintance, there is no need to have people around you who harm you.

There is definitely a limit to what you should put up with from others. Whether as a short-term separation or as a time-out while you redefine the relationship, you may need to put your foot down.

Resilience means being able to be aware of these situations and make choices about who you let into your life and who needs to leave it.

SUPPORTIVE RELATIONSHIPS

Seek Support · Support Others · Boundaries

In this chapter we talked about:

Seek Support

What Keeps Us from Asking for Help – don't be too proud or uncomfortable to ask for help

Why We Should Ask for Help – you need it and others want to give it

How to Ask for Help – follow the simple process to get what you need

Offer Support

How Supporting Others Builds Resilience – you can benefit from focusing on others and the connections you make are valuable

Boundaries

Grudges and Forgiveness – these hurt you more than the other person. Let go of them

Relationship Awareness – notice what is going on in your relationship with others

Redefining Relationships – change the relationship, not the person

For more information please visit:
www.theresilienceway.com

Chapter Seven

Personal Clarity

PERSONAL CLARITY

Personal Values · Personal Vision · Planning

"Can you remember who you were before the world told you who you should be?"

Charles Bukowski

The third Element of Resilience is **Personal Clarity**. Resilience comes from having a clear picture of who you are, what you want in your life, and your plan to achieve your goals.

This Element involves the factor: **Personal Values, Personal Vision and Planning**.

Personal Values is about knowing what MUST be present in your life; those qualities, relationships and ideals that really matter to you. You need to be clear about what is "non-negotiable" for you. When you are clear about your values, you can notice when situations are not in line with them and make appropriate changes.

Your **Personal Vision** is the ultimate picture of what you want to achieve in your life and must be clear so you can align yourself to it. You know the old Yogi Berra quote, "If you don't know where you are going, you might end up someplace else."

This relates exactly to resilience, as we need that view of our direction, so even when times get tough, we have a

177

rudder set for the future. We may be pulled off course by circumstances, but we know where we want to be. That's the power of our **Personal Vision**.

With **Planning** we can reach the goals we envision. Once you have clarity about your **Personal Values** and **Visions**, you need a clear set of goals and a basic plan that will move you forward in step-wise fashion. This is the final factor of **Planning**, which we can generate with some simple skills.

Without **Personal Clarity**, you will be pulled out of alignment when times get tough, and the decisions you make will not be in line with your values or vision. You may not even *know* you are out of alignment, because you did not know where your line was in the first place.

Resilient people use their **Personal Clarity** to steer them through the storm. Adjustments to the plan are made, but awareness of the plan, as well as our values and vison, ensure that any plan adjustments are in line with who we are and what we want in our lives.

Andrea's Story

An example of someone who exemplifies all of the elements of personal clarity is my dear friend Andrea. I met Andrea when I attended an International Women's Day event in a small town near where I lived, when my oldest babe was just a few months old. Andrea ran the local office of a women's support center. I felt an immediate and strong connection to Andrea, as she gave off vibes of sincerity, caring, and warmth. During that day, the call went out for volunteers to help support women in crisis in our community. I joined up right away, partly because the work seemed important, and partly because it offered an opportunity to get to know Andrea. I was not disappointed. As I worked with her, I found her to be a centered, self-aware person who connected with others with openness and honesty.

After a few years, Andrea left the organization she was with and went out on her own, with the intention to make a living as a full-time artist. She and her husband Dan were both artists and were now committed to making this their life's work. And so, they did. I have to say that I have met many, many people over the years, who want to be a full-time (fill in the blank). They might want to be an artist, writer, yoga instructor, and so on. They want to follow their passion. So many of these people never actually do this though.

Why?

Because they lack the resilience of Andrea. They were not sufficiently clear about their dreams; they were not willing to make the commitment. They were not willing to give up the things that were getting in the way of their dream.

Andrea has always shown the ability to know what was right for her. I recall the story of when she met Dan at art school. She apparently took one look at him and knew she was going to love him. Thirty-eight years later, they are still happily together.

When she was not as sure about things, she would use her art, her passion for dance, poetry or nature to allow her to process her feelings and come to the realizations she needed.

I remember that as her two boys got older and more independent, she created several art pieces based on the complex emotions she was feeling as she stepped back as a mother and redefined her relationship to her sons. Her art allowed her to work through her feelings.

When she was undergoing radiation treatments for cancer, Andrea began dancing outside the cancer center after each treatment. This was her way of working through the emotional side of the process.

179

Eventually, there was a flash mob planned in the garden where she danced. Everyone wanted to be part of this process. Andrea had a knack for influencing others with her energy and passion. I danced with her there one day, just the two of us, and I can assure that it was the most natural thing in the world, dancing in the garden as people wandered past. They all smiled, and we smiled.

Andrea had struck again with her ability to connect with people in special and sometimes surprising ways.

Through the clarity of their values, vision and good planning, Andrea and Dan built an art gallery and workshop space where they could work, display and sell their art, and do workshops to teach others their craft. This grew into a successful business and provided space and opportunity for many artists to learn, and then to teach others.

Personal Values

What are Personal Values?

"I have learned that as long as I hold fast to my beliefs and values - and follow my own moral compass - then the only expectations I need to live up to are my own."34

Michelle Obama

Have you ever made a list of the things in your life that are most important to you? What if this list helped you to become and remain clear about what you do and don't want in your life? How would that help? What can you not live without?

Typical values include "focus on family", "honesty" and "trusting relationships", but there is no one set of values. It is less important that you follow any particular set of values, and more important that you are clear about your own personal values.

Integrity comes from knowing yourself and behaving in line with what makes sense to you.

- Values are those things that are most important to you.

- Values change over time. The things that were paramount for you at age twenty are not the same things that are critical at sixty.

- There are no right or wrong values. There are only your values and those that others thrust upon you. Choose to focus on the ones that are truly your own.

- When decisions or situations are not in line with your authentic values, you feel uncomfortable… this a is sign that you need to make a change.

- Clarity about personal values allows you to align your decisions, relationships and life plans with these values.

- Personal values are generally operating in the background of your life, so you are not aware of them until you experience a conflict or difference in values.

How Values Clarity Builds Resilience

What was important to David were his values; supporting people, finding meaningful work, and creating a stable, loving environment for his wife and children. He was a great friend, the kind that spoke the truth, and a great coach to his employees and hockey players. He was always there to lend a hand. He worked hard at his job and enjoyed being good at what he did. He won awards for his success in the bank, and this mattered to him. Above all, the kids and I were his reason for being. We were the reason he got up in the morning, and the reason he fought so hard to stay with us.

David lived these values in his illness and in his dying. He worked right up until his last few months, and if asked how he was doing, even when quite ill, he would report that he was "still working two days a week". This mattered to him. He knew that he had an impact at work and that was important.

David never refused to talk to a friend that called, no matter how tired he might be. He told the same stories over and over again, as each friend called to check in on him. It got to a point where our son, William, who by then had a voice so similar to his Dad's that people would mistake him for his Dad on the phone, offered to take those calls to give his Dad a break. But David just kept on talking to them, no matter how much it took out of him.

The kids and I enjoyed the incredible loyalty of a devoted husband and father. David always put us first. We were his reason for fighting so hard to stay alive. We were his reason to get back on his feet after each round of chemo.

We gave him purpose right up to his last breath. In his last moments, his only noticeable reaction, a "thumbs up", was reserved for the dear friend who told him she would look after us when he was gone. That was all that mattered.

I relied on my own values to help me through the tough times after David passed. My values are family, helping others, learning and growth.

A good friend, who had also lost her first husband at an early age, suggested that if you were accustomed to being in a good, happy marriage, it made sense that you would want that again. It makes sense that you would want to move on, to find a new partner, perhaps sooner than someone for whom marriage had not been such a great experience.

This made sense to me. I missed David, but as I got used to missing him, I became accustomed to this new reality without him. I was aware that I wanted to share my life with someone else in the way I had with David. It was not about replacing David – that can't be done – but I wanted to have a relationship with another person. I knew that I was happier when I had someone to share my life in the special way that you do in a good marriage.

Later, the kids noticed that I was less stressed, as measured by less yelling and anger, once George was on the scene. I was used to having someone to share the parenting, or at least to discuss what should be done with the kids, the household expenses, the farm and all those details. I wanted that again. I wanted adult conversations with someone who knew me well and enjoyed my company in the way a life partner can.

Societal Norms

Clarity of personal values is important because it helps to ensure that you are living your life according to your own values, and not someone else's. For so many of us, differentiating between what is "right" for everyone around us and what actually works for us is difficult. If we are not careful, we end up making everyone else happy, but not ourselves. That is not resilient, and it takes away our opportunity to live up to our potential.

If and when we make choices that don't fully align with our values, we need to know we are doing it, and understand what we are giving up.

As a mom, for instance, I often give up personal time, with the kids' needs taking priority over mine. That's the job, right? But I do recognize when this is happening and find ways to restore my balance. I'm not good for my kids if I don't demonstrate how best to care for oneself.

> "Your time is limited, so don't waste it living someone else's life. Don't be trapped by dogma — which is living with the results of other people's thinking. Don't let the noise of other's opinions drown out your own inner voice. And most important, have the courage to follow your heart and intuition. They somehow already know what you truly want to become. Everything else is secondary."
>
> Steve Jobs

I also ran headlong into societal norms when I became a widow. You may have seen these rules in action. As a widow, we are told not to make any "big" decisions during the first year and to be ready for days of not being able to get out of bed, due to the grief. Society also tells you that there is a clear connection between how long it takes you to move on to a new partner, and how much you loved the one you lost.

Now these rules can be different, and may be more or less constricting, depending on your cultural background and whether you are a man or a woman.

In any event, I was not supposed to meet someone and fall in love within eighteen months of David's passing. But I did. And I knew that David wanted this to happen, because he said so. His values drove him to insist that I "carry on" once he was gone. He told me, on multiple occasions, that I must remarry after he was gone. Above all, he wanted us to be happy.

My values drove me to do what was right for the kids and I, not the judgmental voices around us. After all, I don't have a value called, "do what others' think is okay." My focus on learning and growth had me reading and researching about grief and survival, so I was informed about the choices I was making and could be sure they were sound.

Honestly, I was surprised to be falling in love so soon, but I knew to trust myself, because I knew myself well. I did not allow the opinions of the community to interfere with my decisions.

In this way, I was resilient.

George's First Marriage

Our values don't always lead us in the right direction. Sometimes we need to recognize where our values are getting in our way. This can happen if your values conflict with one another in some way, or do not align to your personal vision.

George stayed in his first marriage far longer than he should have. He had been raised by parents who taught important values like loyalty and being honorable. George's Dad was considered "a true gentleman", a man who did the right thing, spoke the truth, and was dedicated to his family. George is a chip off the old block, and in the case of his unhappy marriage, the thought of leaving never occurred to him.

Subconsciously he was miserable, but his strong attachment to values kept him from being aware of his own mental and emotional state. He was so busy being honorable and loyal that he forgot about being happy. He was sacrificing his happiness and his mental health for the sake of following his values. Without a strong **Personal Vision**, there was nothing to give him the sense that he was out of alignment. And so, he stayed.

By the end, he was depressed and lonely. The trigger happened on the day his wife told him, "I don't love you anymore." This was, for George, a freeing moment. He suddenly realized that he did not want to be in this marriage, either. This loyal, honorable guy had not realized that leaving was an option.

But still, an incredibly difficult journey lay ahead. Going from the end of a miserable marriage to being happy and ready to move on with your life is not an easy process. It certainly was not for George. Again, the values played a part.

> "When the marriage ended, I had to spend a lot of time in self-discovery. I had sacrificed a lot of who I was as a person to accommodate the situation. I had accepted this and, in the process, I forgot who I was. I had to rediscover

myself and what I really wanted to focus on for the rest of my life. I had lost that essence of who I was as a person and had to find it."

George's story helps us learn about noticing how our values are either helping or hindering us. We need to make sure that our values align with what we want in our lives, that they are not driven by the needs or expectations of others, and that they are truly a reflection of what is most important to us. In this way, we can solidify our understanding of our "must-haves" and align our lives accordingly.

Shifting Values

Over time, values change. Sometimes this is a gradual process as we age and gather life experience. In other situations, people have experiences that shift their values more quickly and dramatically. In either case, we need to make sense of the shift in how we see the world.

If you picture the values of the average twenty-year-old, they are significantly different than those of your average sixty-year-old. For instance, most of us, at sixty, value enjoying good health, a condition we probably took for granted at twenty.

When we encounter struggles in our lives, they often have impact on our values. This was the case for George in his divorce. He defines loyalty differently now, and understands how he needs to be loyal to himself, as well as others.

He also defines "honorable" differently, realizing this needs to be defined within the context of what honor means to him personally, rather than what anyone else thinks. It does not mean staying with your wife when doing so is making both of you miserable. Rather, it means finding a way to leave this marriage that is fair, equitable and allows your partner to move on with as little struggle as possible.

George would add a new value to the mix now, that of love and affection. He lives this now through the devotion he shows to his new family. With his special patience and calm approach, he has opened the door to each of our children and allowed each to define a relationship that works for them. It is an interesting and ongoing journey for him and the kids.

In some cases, people have experiences that change their values in a fundamental way, in a short period of time.

I recall reading once about the difficulties that Peace Corps workers have when they return home. They report standing in the grocery store, looking at the endless options in the cereal aisle, and wondering how this scene makes any sense in the context of their experience overseas. They feel lost.

This quote from General Dallaire speaks to this:

> "I found myself increasingly intolerant of home life. I felt frustrated with the children for not wanting to eat their peas or whining for a new toy; I disdained simple requests from my wife to help choose a new sofa pattern or to attend a party with friends; I marvelled at the neighbours washing their cars and pruning their gardens. To me it all seemed so unimportant, so materialistic, so wasteful it was almost obscene."

General Dallaire was forced to relearn his life back in Canada. He had to work out how his values and what really mattered to him had changed. It must have been incredibly difficult when the values of his wife and children had remained the same as always. They had not changed, he had.

188

Resilience means that you have to sort through the implications of these changes and figure out how to live with them as you move forward.

When we have significant life experiences, situations that pull us far out of our comfort zone, whether positive or negative, they change us. They do this partly because our values shift – not in the gradual way they might as we age – but in a fundamental and immediate way. You can't just carry on pretending that the old set of values are still in place, when your experience has taught you that they no longer fit you. This may cause significant discomfort as you adjust, for you and for those around you. Those people who did not share your experience will have no concept of the shift in values you feel. You will need to consider the changes to relationships that may result from this process of shifting values.

Liz's Story

Our daughter, Liz, has been fortunate to go on two "service and learning" trips. The first was to Nicaragua, and then two years later, to Colombia. Her experience in both cases was rich in many ways. Her return home was a struggle.

First, let me explain the trip. It was not a "voluntourism" trip. Those are the ones many Westerners go on, and then come home thinking they have saved the world. They tell stories about what they have seen, how horrible the situation was for those who live there. This supports what we expect, the idea that the West is best. We have it all and the rest of the world needs to catch up.

The trips that Liz was blessed to be a part of were different.

The program, called Two Countries One World (TCOW), had youth spend a year preparing for the trip, learning about the culture of the destination country, and their own. They learned about the struggles of both nations in terms of social issues and culture. They learned about Colombia's history of colonialization and the century-old civil, armed conflict. They learned about the historic peace agreement passed in November 2016, just four months before their trip.

They also learned about Canada's indigenous peoples and the history of Canada's treatment of those indigenous peoples, so that they could develop a more complete understanding of their own country. This was intended to help them reflect on the differences and similarities in the host country.

The group, a dozen youth and their leaders, got to know one another well even before they left. It was an amazing program.

Once in the host countries, Liz lived in a community with the local people for ten days. They shared meals, travelled to other villages, attended religious services and danced the nights away with those who lived in the small community where they were hosted. Very quickly Liz felt connected to the people and the community.

She explained it like this:

> "Living life in a community the way we did made the end come more suddenly than if you were just on vacation. You get used to being there and being with these people. You grow close to these people, and then you feel ripped away. You fall in love with the people because they are so loving and open, you feel a part of the community and close to the youth especially. While you are in the community, connection with people is inevitable, and so, saying goodbye is

190

extremely hard and you don't want to. This connection was so evident the night before we left. The whole community came out and made a circle around us, laying their hands on us and praying for us and our lives; as well as thanking God for bringing us. This was an extremely heightened moment of connection and emotion. Then the next day, you have to leave, which made it all the more difficult. Canada is so distant. It's not that I did not care about home and the people there, but all I wanted to do was stay – so in a way I didn't care."

When the group left from Cartagena, Colombia, with its rich culture and amazing vibrancy, and headed home to Toronto, it was a culture shock. They arrived at Toronto airport and were faced with a crowded terminal filled with people carrying on with their own lives, business people on trips and so on. It was jarring to be surrounded by people who did not understand or care about the experience they had just had.

Then, when they had to leave their group, it was even more difficult because of the connections they had made as a group.

"Family just wants you home and does not understand what you have been through. Teachers and friends ask how your vacation was, or ask how your "crazy, dangerous trip" was. They want to you to confirm what they think... they want your story to be about the "poor unfortunate souls" you met."

But Liz returned with a love for these people, and she would rather be with them, because they are more fortunate in many ways than we are. They live a vibrant life, with immense love toward each other. They have "less" but are happy and satisfied with life.

In Canada we have so many things, but we are not happier. We assume that people in the Global South don't have a satisfied life because they don't have the material possessions we have. Liz's experience taught her that this is just not true. She had met and lived in a community with people who lived full, happy and resilient lives.

> This experience changed Liz's values in many ways.

In some ways, she wants to replicate what she saw in terms of being happy with what you have, and separating happiness from things. She understands that there is no satisfaction in getting more. She appreciates differently the Global South of the world. She wants to share her understanding when she hears people talk with superiority, as if people in the Global South need to become what we are. She sees that all countries are dealing with poverty, gender issues and inequality. Canada has these issues, too. Liz no longer sees the West as the ideal, toward which all others should aspire.

Returning to school after her first trip, at the age of fifteen, was really tough. She did not tell her friends about her experience, as she found that friends wanted to know about really unimportant things; like the cute guys she might have met, which made it more difficult to be home. She found more support from her fellow travelers, who understood her experience and feelings.

This created some distance between her and some of the friends she had at school, but it taught her about the value of keeping a few friends nice and close.

Liz shares:

"I'm a talker, but depending on what I
need to talk about, I find the person I
need. I'm not an open person to
everyone, I have to trust them. When I
need support, I will continue to go to the
person who already knows things about
me and has a similar perspective. I like
to talk to someone who will listen, and
then give input and advice, perhaps
sharing a different perspective. I have
also learned to be a support for others,
and I feel a hopefulness when I can help
other people. As I give and receive this
support, I build trust with people. My
circle is not huge, but these are people
who have earned my trust. They are the
ones I go back to again and again."

You can hear that Liz's values, as learned and
solidified on her trips, are strong and clear to her. She has a
much better sense of self, and what matters to her as a result
of these experiences. She had to make sense of the shifts in
her understanding of the world when she returned home.
The process of relearning has made her more confident and
ready to take on new challenges. In this way, she is more
resilient.

Values Alignment

For some people, the issue of personal values is not
one of losing track of your values, but of needing to align
behavior to your espoused values. Once we know our values,
we need to find those situations where we are not living them,
and make changes. We can't build resilience in situations

where the decisions we are making or accepting are not in alignment with our values.

If, for instance, your values call for you to put your family first, to make them a priority, then that job you have that takes you away from your family far too often has to go. You need to make a change. If honesty is a key value for you, then you can't continue to avoid those difficult conversations with someone who is unaware that they are causing you harm. You have to be honest!

David aligned his behavior to his values on a regular basis. He worked hard, but he was always ready to run the kids to hockey practice on time. At a young age, they learned to pack their equipment and be standing at the door, as Dad would run in and grab the kid and hockey bag, kiss the wife, and be back on the road. When a friend needed help, he dropped what he was doing and helped. When friends and family were taken care of, he poured himself into his work and enjoyed much success in his career. In this way, he was true to his values.

Resilience lies in knowing what values matter to you, and then aligning your behavior to these values. Understanding your values will also help you to decide on your Personal Vision, the next Factor in The Resilience Way™.

Personal Vision

"What man actually needs is not a tensionless state but rather the striving and struggling for a worthwhile goal, a freely chosen task. What he needs is not the discharge of tension at any cost but the call of a potential meaning waiting to be fulfilled by him." 35

This quote by Viktor E. Frankl, the renowned psychiatrist and author of *Man's Search for Meaning*, talks to the power of a Personal Vision. We can survive our difficulties and be truly resilient when we have a clear picture of what we want to accomplish. We need a calling.

What is a Personal Vision?

We need to have a clear, vivid, imaginative picture in our minds of where we are going and what it will look like when we get there. We need to be able to imagine a point in the future when we will have achieved what we want most in our lives.

This is your **Personal Vision**.

Think about your **Personal Vision** and articulate:

- Where you will be

- Who will be there

- What you will have accomplished

- How you will feel

This vision needs to be compelling so that we feel driven to make it happen... every day!

How Your Personal Vision Builds Resilience

You have heard some form of the expression: "if you don't know where you are going, any road will get you there." It is often attributed to the Cheshire Cat in Lewis Carroll's, *Alice's Adventures in Wonderland.* It is actually from the George Harrison song, *Any Road.*

This confusion is understandable because the phrase relates so closely to the following exchange between Alice and the Cheshire Cat:[36]

> "Would you tell me, please, which way I ought to go from here?"
>
> "That depends a good deal on where you want to get to," said the Cat.
>
> "I don't much care where—" said Alice.
>
> "Then it doesn't matter which way you go," said the Cat.
>
> "—so long as I get SOMEWHERE," Alice added as an explanation.
>
> "Oh, you're sure to do that," said the Cat, "if you only walk long enough."

For many people, this is how they live their lives. They don't have any idea where they are headed, so any action they take, any decision they make, is as good as any other. They make decisions based on the needs of others and choose paths that lead them in random directions. They return to old patterns based on what is comfortable and safe, or least not difficult.

> In the end, they are not happy
> about the outcome of their actions,
> but they don't see what went wrong.

It's a matter of not being clear about their vision. They did not know what they wanted to create in their lives, and so anything they created seemed fine. If Alice keeps walking, she will end up somewhere, doing something, with someone. She will end up fulfilling a vision of some kind. Just not her own vision.

The difference between people who live their vision and those who don't is often a matter of clarity. Those who know where they want to go have a good chance of getting there, just by virtue of this clarity. Alice needs to know what she is called to do, her dream for herself, what she is driven to do.

David had a clear vision for his life before he got sick. His vision was to be a great dad, husband and friend. He wanted to live a life that would make his loved ones proud. Once David was diagnosed with stage four colon cancer, his vision shifted, but not that much. His new vision was to keep his family life as stable as possible, while he fought off the disease that was threatening to kill him. His long-term vision had not changed. He was still planning on surviving and continuing to be a great dad, husband and friend.

Once the doctors said that he had only three months to live, his vision shifted once more. His vision, at that point, was to live as long as possible, and to tidy up as many loose ends as he could, so that his passing would be as easy as possible on his children, his wife and his friends. Hence, his "to-do" list for after he was gone, his funeral arrangements which were made as soon as his death was a certainty, and his designing of his headstone, in order to ensure this too did not become a burden on me after he was gone.

Throughout this difficult process, David's personal vision shifted, but remained a strong part of his method for staying grounded and carrying on. It was a key part of his resiliency.

> My vision has always been to live out my dreams and to help others to do the same.

At the end of my life, I hope that people will say that I did what I wanted to, lived my life on my own terms, and was helpful to my family, friends and the others I met along the way. I want to be good for the world. I have been living this vision for as long as I can remember.

I recall that as a young person, I knew I wanted to live in the country, I wanted to be self-employed, and I wanted a family. This has always made sense to me.

When David got sick, my vision did not change. It did, however, guide how I wanted to behave while he was sick. I wanted to help. I wanted to hold my family together. I wanted to support all the people affected by his illness.

My "dream" became about getting through his illness with the children experiencing as little trauma as possible. It was about getting to the other side of cancer as a family.

This vision kept me grounded in thinking about the needs of David, the kids, other family members and friends. It kept me from becoming focused on my own suffering, my own worries. It supported my resilience. As we got closer to the end, nothing changed about my vision. My focus became more on David's care and the care of our children.

For a time, my work fell to the wayside. I was doing what I needed to do.

When David became sick, I was in the process of running and growing my consulting practice. I continued to work throughout most of his illness, as my work was supporting our family, plus continuing the work that I love was good for me.

If my vision for my work hadn't been clear, it might have been tempting to look for a job with a company that would provide a more stable and certain income. But I knew myself; and I knew that I needed my work to give me strength. No matter what happened, I needed to carry on with my own intellectual and career pursuits, as best I could.

I did not work for the last five months of David's life. I told my key clients that I would be taking some time off. I had no specific plans for my return to work and spent those five months hanging out with David. We were like an old retired couple. We did the grocery shopping, went out for lunch, and went to his medical appointments. I was not thinking about work.

At David's funeral, I was surprised to see three of my key clients in attendance. They shared their condolences like all the other attendees. They also said that I should contact them as soon as I was ready.

At the time, I could have said, "Ready for what?" I was that far from thinking about my work. But after a week or so passed, it occurred to me that I should touch base with these folks, just to see what's new. They all shared that they had work they were holding off on, awaiting my return. They had held off on training and development projects so that I could do them when I was ready! I was shocked. It was not what I was expecting.

I gave myself three weeks to get my personal affairs in order before I returned to my training and coaching practice. It was a wonderful distraction and a great way to feel that I could return to the real world and be helpful to others in a different way than I did at home. Talking business and leadership was a welcome distraction.

I know that keeping my long-term goals in place helped me to understand that going back to work was the right move. I also knew that taking a break from work for five months was a necessary pause.

Clarity of personal values, vision and goals was my rudder in a stormy sea. My vision allowed me to feel confident in all of those decisions and live without regret, since I know I have been true to my dreams.

Trauma and difficulty can have the effect of helping us to focus on our vision.

For some people, a tough life creates an obvious path. There seems to be only one option; and it is to make some significant change to the situation they face. They don't need to search for vision, it finds them.

They do, however, have to pick up the torch.

They demonstrate their resilience in their willingness to follow the obvious path, no matter how difficult the journey might be, or what they might have to give up in the process.

Nelson Mandela

"During my lifetime I have dedicated myself to this struggle of the African people. I have fought against white domination, and I have fought against black domination. I have cherished the ideal of a democratic and free society in which all persons live together in harmony and with equal opportunities. It is an ideal which I hope to live for and to achieve. But if needs be, it is an ideal for which I am prepared to die."37

This quote was shared in Nelson Mandela's statement from the dock at his trial for sabotage in 1964. In it, he shows his clarity of vision, of what he wanted to achieve and what he was willing to do to get there. At the time, it must have seemed like an uphill battle, but it was one he dedicated the rest of his life to fighting.

At the time of Mandela's trial for treason, Hendrik Verwoerd, a Dutch-born South African politician, sociologist and journalist served as the prime minister of South Africa, and continued as its prime minister from 1961 until his assassination in 1966. His goal was to preserve minority rule by white Afrikaners over the various non-white ethnic groups, who were the majority of South Africa's population. To that end, he greatly expanded apartheid, the system of forced classification and segregation by race that existed in South Africa from 1948 to 1994.

Verwoerd considered apartheid as merely "good-neighborliness", but it caused almost the entire non-white population of South Africa to be excluded, lose civil rights, and suffer discrimination. Verwoerd heavily repressed anti-apartheid activism and banned organizations like the African National Congress (ANC) and the Pan Africanist Congress (PAC).

After twenty-seven years in prison, having used this time to further his cause and continue to work for equality, Mandela was released and went on to become the President of South Africa from 1994 to 1999.

In his 1994 autobiography, he had this to say about his life's work:

"I was not born with a hunger to be free. I was born free-free in every way that I could know. Free to run in the fields near my mother's hut, free to swim in the clear stream that ran through my village, free to roast mealies under the stars and ride the broad backs of slow-moving bulls. As long as I obeyed my father and abided by the customs of my tribe, I was not troubled by the laws of man or God. It was only when I began to learn that my boyhood freedom was an illusion, when I discovered as a young man that my freedom had already been taken from me, that I began to hunger for it. At first, as a student, I wanted freedom only for myself, the transitory freedoms of being able to stay out at night, read what I pleased, and go where I chose. Later, as a young man in Johannesburg, I yearned for the basic and honorable freedoms of achieving my potential, or earning my keep, of marrying and having a family-the freedom not to be obstructed in a lawful life. But then I slowly saw that not only was I not free, but my brothers and sisters were not free. I saw that it was not just my freedom that was curtailed, but the freedom of everyone who looked like I did. That is when I joined the African National Congress, and that is when the hunger for my own freedom became the greater hunger for the freedom of my people. It was this desire for the freedom of my people to live their lives with dignity and self-respect that animated my life, that transformed a frightened young man into a bold one, that drove a law-abiding attorney to become a criminal, that turned a family-loving husband into a man without a home, that forced a life-loving man to live like a monk. I am no more virtuous or self-sacrificing than the next man, but I found that I could not even enjoy the poor and limited freedoms I was allowed when I knew my people were not free. Freedom is indivisible; the chains on any one of my people were the chains on all of them, the chains on all of my people were the chains on me. It was during those long and lonely years that my hunger for the freedom of my own people became a hunger for the freedom of all people, white and black. I knew as well as I knew anything that the oppressor must be liberated just as surely as the oppressed. A man who takes away another man's freedom is a prisoner of hatred, he is locked behind the bars of prejudice and narrow-mindedness. I am not truly free if I am taking away someone else's freedom, just as surely as I am not free when my freedom is taken from me. The oppressed and the oppressor alike are robbed of their humanity. When I walked out of prison, that was my mission, to liberate the oppressed and the oppressor both. Some say that has now been achieved. But I know that that is not the case. The truth is that we are not yet free; we have merely achieved the freedom to be free, the right not to be oppressed. We have not taken the final step of our journey, but the first step on a longer and even more difficult road. For to be free is not merely to cast off one's chains, but to live in a way that respects and enhances the freedom of others. The true test of our devotion to freedom is just beginning. I have walked that long road to freedom. I have tried not to falter; I have made missteps along the way. But I have discovered the secret that after climbing a great hill, one only finds that there are many more hills to climb. I have taken a moment here to rest, to steal a view of the glorious vista that surrounds me, to look back on the distance I have come. But I can rest only for a moment, for with freedom comes responsibilities, and I dare not linger, for my long walk is not yet ended."38

Creating Your Own Struggle

If we want to live our dreams or work toward our vision, we need to struggle. Nothing great was ever easy. Your vision should challenge you so that you are learning and stretching.

That stretching – or struggle – builds resilience. It teaches you that you can do more than you thought possible, that you can work through the difficult moments and find success. When we do this well, we create a vision that is achievable, but a stretch, and we reap the rewards in personal growth.

Terry Fox

One of the best examples of someone who created his own struggle is Canada's own Terry Fox. This young man was only 18 when he was diagnosed with bone cancer and had his right leg amputated. While in hospital, he was so deeply concerned about the other cancer patients he met and their suffering, he decided to begin fund-raising efforts. This led to him beginning the "Marathon of Hope", which involved running across our enormous country in order to raise money for cancer research. He prepared for a year and a half and began his run on April 12, 1980. He ran twenty-six miles a day for 143 days. He ran through the maritime provinces long before summer arrived. It was cold, wet and windy. He was incredibly determined. According to Terry:

> "There can be no reason for me to stop.
> No matter what pain I suffer, it is nothing
> compared to the pain of those who have
> cancer, of those who endure treatment."

He ran through 3339 miles before he was forced to stop running because cancer had appeared in his lungs. He passed away on June 28, 1981, at the age or twenty-two.

Since Terry's death, Canadians have carried on his dream and each year we hold runs all over the country to raise money. To date, over $750 million dollars has been raised in his name.

Terry did not have to do any of this. He could have focused on continuing his life as an average teenager. He could have just gone back to his life and tried to forget about his cancer. Instead, he took on an enormous challenge that gave his life more meaning and significance than one could imagine. His impact on the world has been enormous, especially given his short life. His decision to create a struggle and to work toward an important goal, continues to inspire us today. He had a vision to help others. This is truly an example of a resilient young man.

> "There is nothing in the world, I venture to say, that would so effectively help one to survive even the worst conditions as the knowledge that there is a meaning in one's life."39
>
> Viktor E Frankl

Non-Attachment to Outcome

Our vision does not need to be written in stone. It is not intended to be unmovable. At different points in your life your vision will change. As it should. Life changes, as you know all too well – and so, your vision will as well.

I have found that there is an elegance to creating vision, a complexity that can be at times fascinating, at other times concerning.

And at some point, I began to love the term "non-attachment to outcome". This was when I realized that all of my life lessons, up until that point, had been about setting and achieving goals without fail. I was always reaching for the next, greater achievement. I finished my undergrad with a complete focus on getting into an M.B.A. program. I finished the M.B.A. with a focus on landing a great job. I worked the job, eighty hours a week, in order to get a promotion.

I had developed strong skills in accomplishing things, and a weak ability to enjoy the process along the way. To say

I did not often "stop to smell the roses" was an understatement.

The idea of non-attachment to outcome became a confusing and fascinating learning process.

I began to notice that although there were still many areas of my life where goal-setting was important, there were several where goal-setting was getting in the way. Always focusing on the next milestone was stopping me from enjoying my successes. It was also stopping me from making use of my intuitive side. It forced a logical process on everything I did. It encouraged me to only look externally for evidence of my success, with no internal focus at all.

I had become out of touch with myself.

Non-attachment to outcome became a mantra because it helped me to consider which areas of my life required goal-setting, and which should be allowed to flow on their own, no matter the direction.

It was at this time I also became a fan of the expression:

"the universe gives you what you need,
when you need it."

Without attachment to a specific goal, I found that I was more open to signals the universe was sending. I could be open to consider the multitude of ways that I could reach my overall vision.

In some areas of my life, this openness had enormous impact. My goal-driven approach had made me terrible at certain things.

For instance, I was not a good listener. I was impatient. I gave advice instead of listening, and I felt pressure to be able to solve other people's problems. When I learned to listen without attachment, I could be fully present in the conversation. I no longer felt the desperate need to have all the answers. I could just be a sounding board. Non-attachment also allowed me to explore new areas of my life without the concern for being good at anything, or succeeding in any particular way.

This led me into the world of art and allowed me to become an "artist".

This became a gift with implications I could not foresee, as my children watched me and followed along with confidence that being an artist is not something unusual or unattainable. Through my actions, I taught them that if you enjoy being creative and making art, then you are an artist. Three out of four are talented artists, the other is a football coach. I'm sure there is art in football, I just don't understand enough about the game to see it.

So, by maintaining some freedom, by allowing my goals to exist without the route to them being certain, and by being comfortable with that ambiguity, I have learned that things can be better than I ever imagined.

I am comfortable that I have not missed too many opportunities because I was too narrowly focused and could not see all the possibilities. I have also tried to pass this on to those around me, so they can see their own possibilities.

Non-attachment has had impact on my parenting as well. I have set goals with my children and taught them about the importance of working toward your goals. But I have also taught them to remain open to other possibilities and to notice what the universe is bringing.

So many times, for instance, I have encouraged them to try something new, something in which they have an interest, but not any experience. I have told them to try out for a team, try a new hobby, and then, trust that, eventually, they will know if this new thing is for them. I have not encouraged them to stick to things that don't feel right, but to focus on where they feel passion.

At times, this has led them to do things I didn't choose or would not choose, but that's when non-attachment comes into play. I can't know what is right for my children all the time. They have to develop the skill of learning what makes them happy, fulfills their passions, and therefore, makes them resilient. My children need to find their own path, find clarity in their own personal vision, and set goals that will get them there.

When my son was a baby, I did not hope that he would become a football coach. Luckily, I did demonstrate that he should follow his passion and his dreams, and now I have the extreme pleasure of watching him do what he loves. Oh, and by the way, he is impacting on the lives of young players in ways that fit with my passion for helping people. In the end, I could not ask for more than to have my son living his dreams and having a positive impact on the world.

> As life catches you along the way, bringing struggles, you can – with your overall goal in mind, manage to still move forward through the tough times and build the life you want.

Personal vision is key to resilience.

No matter whether your vision is to be a good parent or friend, or to change the world, clarity around what you want to accomplish will keep you grounded. You decide what your vision should be. You figure out what your dreams look like, and then, hold fast to that vision until it becomes a reality.

With a clear Personal Vision, you are also able begin the process of putting a plan in place to move yourself in the direction of your vision.

Wild Geese

You do not have to be good.

You do not have to walk on your knees

For a hundred miles through the desert, repenting.

You only have to let the soft animal of your body

love what it loves.

Tell me about despair, yours, and I will tell you mine.

Meanwhile the world goes on.

Meanwhile the sun and the clear pebbles of the rain

are moving across the landscapes,

over the prairies and the deep trees,

the mountains and the rivers.

Meanwhile the wild geese, high in the clean blue air,

are heading home again.

Whoever you are, no matter how lonely,

the world offers itself to your imagination,

calls to you like the wild geese, harsh and exciting --

over and over announcing your place

in the family of things.

Mary Oliver

Planning

What is Planning?

You may be aware of what you want to have in your life, but you can't seem to make it happen. Perhaps things keep getting in your way? Do you ever wonder what your life would be like if you did not have so many constraints; like money, family commitments, education, or time?

In order to succeed we need to have clearly defined plans that take us, step-by-step, from where we are to where we want to be. Our plan must link directly to our **Personal Vision**, as these are the steps required to achieve that vision.

> In the absence of a plan, of course, nothing changes.

How Planning Builds Resilience

Planning is how we get from where we are, no matter where that is, to where we want to be. There is no point in having a clear picture of where you want to end up (your vision), if you can't put the steps in place to get there. Many people have big dreams, but never seem to be moving toward them. Good goal setting and action planning are the tools we use to make sure our dreams become a reality.

I have met people over the years who feel that setting goals is a waste of time because life can be so uncertain and setting goals is therefore useless. In my experience this has not been true. Resilient people build plans to ensure they can navigate even when the waters get rough. Without a plan you are sure to fail. With a plan you have a starting point from which to build contingencies and work your way through the difficulty.

How to Plan

Planning involves two things: setting goals and creating an action plan to achieve the goals.

Some goals will be short term; others longer. All goals should be specific enough to support clarity, and involve a measurable timeframe. Writing down goals, with timelines, is an important step in making them come to life.

Action plans help you reach your goals step-by-step and are a critical part of the planning process. If you don't know what steps are necessary to get to your goal, and don't have those steps planned out, you are unlikely to get there.

If this is beginning to sound complicated, let's be clear, it is not. Here is a simple flowchart of how it works:

Goal	Action Steps	Completion Date
• What you want to accomplish • How you will know when you get there (measurement)	Specific action steps you will take	Date by which the action step will be complete

Example: For a goal set January 1, 2025		
I want to move from this apartment into a house that I own. I will do this within the next five years.	• Assess and document my current financial situation	Feb 1, 2025
	• Create a realistic budget showing how I can save for a down payment	Feb 15, 2025
	• Follow the budget and track any deviation from the budget	Feb 15, 2025 through June 30, 2029
	• Begin the house search	June 30, 2029
	• Move into my new house	By January 1, 2030

Adjusting Plans When Times Get Tough

The goals you set in your stable times help to keep you centered when times get tough. Having set those initial goals informs how you will alter them when circumstances change. Re-setting your goals in uncertain times is useful, because it allows you to control as much as you can. You may have very little control, but at least you are using what you have.

When we go through difficulties that alter our lives, we have to think about how this impacts our plans. You may know the story of Sheryl Sandberg, author and COO of Facebook, who lost her husband after he suffered a sudden heart attack. Her book, *Option B,* explores this experience and how she and her two young children moved forward after this tragedy. She shares an important thought about moving forward:

> "Although it can be extremely difficult to grasp, the disappearance of one possible self can free us to imagine a new possible self. After tragedy, we sometimes miss these opportunities because we spend all of our emotional energy wishing for our old lives."40

Sheryl learned, as we all need to, that we can and must move forward and alter our plans as we go. When something difficult happens, we have the opportunity to look at new possibilities and decide on a new path. This is not easy; and it takes time to see the situation in this way. We are resilient when we see these opportunities and create new plans based on them.

Luck and The Universe

Have you ever met someone who thinks that everything happens due to luck? When good things happen, they were lucky. When bad things happen, luck was against them. I've even met people who play the victim card and blame luck. These people take no responsibility for the outcome, assuming that the negative outcomes have nothing to do with their own decisions and actions – it's all just bad luck.

I think a good way to think about luck is through the ancient quote: "Luck favors the prepared." By being focused on a goal and having a plan in place to reach it, you allow luck to find you. You allow the elements into your life that will help you. You recognize them when they arrive. You don't miss huge opportunities because you had no idea they were meant for you.

For me, luck relates back to the powers of the universe sending you what you need. However, you need to be able to recognize the elements that are meant for you. "Luck", in other words, requires that you have a plan in place, so you can notice the elements that will help you, grab hold of them, and use them in your plan.

Dr. Wayne Dyer

You may be familiar with the work of this brilliant man. I was exposed to it in my early adulthood and it is the basis of my thoughts of how I interact with the universe. Dr. Dyer, in his many books and presentations, shares a way of thinking about how clarity of values, vision and planning allow us to tap into the power of the universe. It is from him that I got my mantra, "the universe sends me what I need, when I need it."

He puts it much more eloquently when he says:

> "Everything in the universe has a purpose. Indeed, the invisible intelligence that flows through everything in a purposeful fashion is also flowing through you."

The purpose of knowing yourself, what you want and where you are headed, is to ensure that when things that you need come along, you recognize them. In this way, you build your vision. In this way, you become your best self, your most resilient self.

Personal Clarity is about creating a solid understanding of what matters to you, what you want to accomplish in your life, and how you plan to get there. With this understanding, you can better manage your life in good times and through difficulty. This clarity allows you to adjust your pathway, to allow for welcome surprises and new challenges. You never know what will happen to you in life, but better to prepare for success on your own terms, and then, adjust as needed so that you achieve your **Personal Vision**.

PERSONAL CLARITY

Personal Values · Personal Vision · Planning

In this chapter we talked about:

Personal Values

Societal Norms – don't worry about anyone else's values, just your own

Shifting Values – your values will change over time and that's okay

Values Alignment – are you behaving in line with your values?

Personal Vision

What is Your Personal Vision – can you articulate what you want to accomplish in your life?

Creating Your Own Struggle – plan for things that are a stretch goal for you

Non-Attachment to Outcome – allow openness so that you can respond to changes as they come, both good and bad

Planning

How to Plan – the process is simple, doing it is critical

Adjusting When Times Get Tough – your plan will change, that's okay

Luck and The Universe – when you have a plan, you can take advantage of unexpected gifts that pass your way

For more information please visit:
www.theresilienceway.com

Chapter Eight

Dynamic Thinking

DYNAMIC THINKING

Confidence · Realism · Learning Focus

> "We cannot solve our problems with the same thinking we used when we created them."
>
> Albert Einstein

The next Element of Resilience is **Dynamic Thinking**. Once you have a clear direction gained through clarity of your personal values, vision and goals, you are ready to move forward and implement your plan. You need to have the skills and a mindset that will enable you to work through difficulties as you encounter them. This is **Dynamic Thinking**.

This Element involves the factors: **Confidence, Realism and Learning Focus**.

Confidence involves your need to know that you will succeed. You need **confidence** so that you will persevere when the road gets rough. Confidence is about optimism, being able to see the possibilities before you, and not being pulled down by possible risks, or your fears and worries.

Realism is the ability to objectively look at what is helping and hindering your progress. You need to be able to see situations realistically, so that you can notice what is getting in your way.

221

Learning Focus allows you to make significant and permanent changes to ensure you succeed. Once you know what is not working, you need to be able to learn and adapt to situations and make changes to your habits and behavior that move you in the direction of your goals.

Resilient people can adapt and change in order to accomplish their goals. They do not remain stuck in old patterns and have the confidence that they can make things work. This means they effectively put one foot in front of the other until they get to their end point.

Confidence

"Everything you need you already have. You are complete right now, you are a whole, total person, not an apprentice person on the way to someplace else. Your completeness must be understood by you and experienced in your thoughts as your own personal reality."

Wayne Dyer

What is Confidence?

The dictionary definition of confidence is:

> "belief in oneself and one's powers or a
> bilities; self-confidence; self-
> reliance; assurance."

Having confidence is about knowing you can and will succeed. This is not about thinking you are better than other people, but about thinking you are worthy. Confidence is an attitude that allows you to see the possibilities in front of you and not be pulled down by the possible risks.

We develop confidence in many ways. New knowledge and learning gives us confidence. Proven knowledge gives us confidence. Proven abilities give us confidence. Tested skills with positive results give us confidence. From there, we are armed, know ourselves and our abilities, and can be confident in taking on challenges.

It is about knowing you can set goals for yourself that you can reach. It is about trusting that you have or can develop the skills you need to overcome obstacles. As in Dr. Dyer's quote, you need to know in your heart that you have what you need to succeed.

How Confidence Builds Resilience

Without confidence, you are missing the energy you need to move forward. With confidence, you have a sense that you can accomplish your goals and can work through the issues that get in the way. This positive attitude allows you to look more objectively at the struggles you face.

A confident person is also a hopeful person, a person who does not get bogged down in the fear of what could go wrong, and instead, problem solves to make things happen.

223

On the day I read Roméo Dallaire's book, *Waiting for First Light, My Ongoing Battle with PTSD,* I also emailed General Dallaire via his website, asking him to have a cup of coffee with me. I wanted to discuss how resilience and PTSD were related. I wanted his thoughts on how his experience relates to the struggles we all face.

This is a retired three-star General with the Canadian military. Part of me was thinking, "Why would he talk to me?" My resilient side, however, simply thought that he might agree to talk. He is, after all, just another human being who knows what it's like to want to connect to someone else, and he might find time for me.

I also thought that there was nothing to lose by asking. He might not agree to the meeting, but then, I was no farther behind, was I?

In fact, he did say "No", sort of. What I received in reply was a warmly worded email from his Executive Director, letting me know that the General was not doing interviews, and wishing me well on my book. I then asked if I could send along what I was writing about the General, in order to ensure I got it right. The next email confirmed that this would be fine.

In the end I got what I needed, the chance to share my work with this amazing man, and to make sure I did not offend him in any way with my remarks. If this help ends up coming solely from his Executive Director, an accomplished writer herself, I'm good with that.

My confidence that this book I'm writing matters, and that I can make it happen, allows me to think abundantly and look for opportunities, rather than assume they are beyond my reach.

> "Inaction breeds doubt and fear. Action breeds confidence and courage. If you want to conquer fear, do not sit home and think about it. Go out and get busy."
>
> Dale Carnegie

Confidence was also a key part of our journey through David's illness. We had two points around which we were confident: he had a chance of survival despite the odds and, no matter what happened, we would be able to handle it. To be honest, I did not think in detail about how I would handle the worst possible outcome, until that outcome became inevitable. Nevertheless, I knew we could handle it.

Keeping a Positive Attitude

A friend of mine, who survived a war before emigrating to Canada, feels that his resilience is strongly linked to keeping a positive attitude, even in the worst situations. This is what he related to me:

> "I think it's important to find anything that is good in a situation. Situations can be very bad, but in order to fight it, we need to find the positive things in it."

He continues, "Every day we hear bad news. In fact, it seems that only bad news makes the news. Just turn on the TV and you'll see war here, immigration crisis there, shooting at home, lost jobs, sanctions, nuclear weapons. Even the weather channel is similar. For example, if the weather is good for the next ten days, then they go all over the world to see where there are storms and wildfires. If the week is so quiet and they have nothing bad to report, they will go to the archives and will tell you that, 'on this day in 1987 there was a huge storm cutting down power and destroying houses...' That all creates a situation where our day is filled with all this negative information and our attitude becomes negative as a result. We feel like we are not in control of our situation...

> "Whenever I found myself in a bad situation, I was always saying to myself: "I've seen way worse than this in my life and I will get out of this, too. It is very important to think about the positives and to keep a positive attitude about everybody and everything. I wish everyone well. And I don't just say that, I really mean it."

This is very wise advice from someone who has survived more trauma than most. You can't focus on past trauma; you have to move forward with faith that there are good things ahead.

> "Our greatest glory is not in never falling, but in rising every time we fall."
>
> Confucius

A Leap of Faith

Being able to do something, even when you are not sure it will work out, is key to resilience.

"I wanted a perfect ending. Now I've learned, the hard way, that some poems don't rhyme, and some stories don't have a clear beginning, middle and end. Life is about not knowing, having to change, taking the moment and making the best of it, without knowing what's going to happen next."

Gilda Radner

You need to be able to listen to the voice in your head that says, "Go for it!" You need to trust that a positive outcome is not only possible, but probable, and that if it does not work out, you will still learn something that will help you to succeed in the future.

That's taking "a leap of faith" and it is a key part of resilience. You need to keep your eye on the goal you have set, celebrate the success you have already enjoyed, and jump.

I did this when I met George, eventually. I often joke that George was "handed to me on a silver platter" and in some ways this is a fairly accurate description. My friend Kimberley, who is in the habit of looking for ways to help other people, noticed that she had two friends, who were both single. She decided to solve this "problem".

In my case, it was really not a problem, because this was just over a year after David died and I was not really thinking that I was ready to move on – yet.

George, on the other hand, had expressed an interest in meeting someone new.

227

Kimberley began by making a list of three people each of us could try dating, and then she told George he should be dating me. She told him I was perfect for him. She convinced him that he should come to her house for dinner, that she and her husband Mike would host George and I for dinner.

When he agreed, she called me. I said, "No". Then I said, "It seems like that would be really awkward." Eventually, I said, "Okay." It's hard to say "No" to Kimberley. She has a habit of getting her way.

We had dinner at Kimberley and Mike's place. It was the most uncomfortably awkward experience I can recall. It was like there was the proverbial "elephant in the room," the huge thing that no one was talking about. We still had a good time, as Kimberley and Mike are good company, but at the end of the evening George and I stood in the driveway together, agreed that this was a really awkward experience and said goodnight. Neither of us felt a desperate need to meet again.

But Kimberley was not done with us yet. She called George and told him he needed to ask me out to dinner. Her argument was that he needed more friends anyway, and I would make a good friend. She then called me and asked, "If George asked you out to dinner, would you say yes?" I thought about it a bit and said that I would. And so, we planned a dinner.

I recall driving to the dinner. I was nervous that he would be so quiet that I would have to do all the talking. I was nervous about going on a "date". I had really never dated in my life. My girlfriend Terri tried to put an end to my nervousness with her usual realism, "You have to eat dinner anyway." Funny times!

So, George and I sat down together in a nice restaurant, one of our favorites now, and started to talk.

This is where the leap of faith began.

I started the evening with the following explanation: "I just want to say that this is NOT a date. I'm not sure what this is, perhaps just dinner, but it's not a date. I don't date. I have never dated. I had bliss before, with my late husband, and I know I will find that again. I trust the universe to bring me what I need, when it is the right time. So, I have no idea how this will go, but it's definitely not a date."

Now, in case you are thinking, "there's no way she said that…", I want you to know that I checked the quote with George and that is also what he remembers. He says that he was really wondering what we were doing, if not going on a date. He was a little worried.

The point is that my discomfort with "dating" was palpable. I needed to explain, as best I could, how I was feeling. It felt authentic. I was not trying to be perfect, or "datable". I took a leap of faith that things would work out. I was not attached to my new "bliss" being with this particular man. It was our first "dinner", after all. I just had faith that things would work out.

George, by the way, had his own funny moments that night. He shared his "list" with me. It was quite funny, really. He counted them off on his fingers as he said, "I need my next wife to be independent, want to travel, have children, drink coffee and wine, and be pretty". It sounded a bit like a job description. A good job though.

The dinner went wonderfully and we talked for hours. When we stood outside and said good night, we both knew we would see each other again.

Two more dinners, many more hours of talking and we were in love. It was that easy. It was a leap of faith by two people who just had to trust that being authentic with one another would either lead to great love, or a great new friend. I'm so glad it turned into another wonderful love story. It's still hard for me to believe that one woman could find two amazing men, in one lifetime.

Although taking a leap of faith when finding love seems scary enough, for many people there is much more on the line. For my friend Cindy, the stakes were much higher for her and her family. And yet they leapt…

Cindy's Story

Cindy was born in Northern Vietnam during the "Resistance War against America". That's the one we in the west call, "The Vietnam War." When the war was over, her family struggled to survive and her father talked about wanting to leave. Her mother did not want to leave, as she was afraid of the danger involved in trying to escape. Finally, after many heated arguments, Cindy's father won her over. A plan was eventually made for the entire family, her parents, an aunt and uncle and cousin, her brother and his wife, to cross the water into China.

On the night of their escape, they walked for half an hour in the dark to get to four boats that they had prepared for the journey. At one point in their journey, they had to double back to find Cindy's mother and cousin, who had become separated from the group in the darkness. After finding them, they all got to the boats and sailed in these small vessels out onto the water.

As the sun came up, they realized that they were not far enough from land. They could see soldiers with guns on the shore. For some reason, they did not shoot though, and allowed the group to continue their journey.

Eventually, they landed on the Chinese coast, where they stayed for two months. They then climbed back into the four boats and began a journey along the coast, heading for Hong Kong, where they understood it would be possible to find their way to other parts of the world.

Along the way they paid to join another larger boat, with the understanding that this boat would move much faster than they could on their own. They got onto this vessel, which already had two hundred people aboard, only to find that it was not faster and the inhabitants of this boat were fighting.

When the family arrived in Hong Kong, they lived in a refugee camp for two years. The camp was horribly crowded and dirty. A shower intended for bathing required you to stand in dirty water up to your ankles.

The Vietnamese in this camp were not getting along as those from the North felt that those from the South had sold the country to the Americans. In the end, the camp split into two groups.

After two years, the family was sponsored by Canadians to go to Newfoundland. They were so grateful to these people for giving them a safe place to make a new beginning.

Cindy moved with her parents, her brother and his wife to Newfoundland and enjoyed freedom for the first time. Other family members eventually settled in Toronto and Seattle. Cindy's family eventually moved to Toronto, to be closer to family there.

Cindy met her husband in Toronto. He had been raised in Southern Vietnam and also experienced the horrors of war. These two amazing people now live in a small town in Ontario with their four children. They are grateful for what Canada has provided. Their children are free and happy Canadians, who will never know the terrible situations their parents survived. Cindy and her husband work happily, six days a week, to provide for their family.

When Cindy thinks about what got her through all those horrific days before she came to Canada, she says:

> "It's simple… HOPE! I had hope that a better life awaited me. Nothing more."

Hope

I was at a conference in Chicago and chatting about my book with my friend Deb Calvert. I was explaining that I needed to learn more about hope, that I was concerned that the term was bandied about too easily as a catch-all, and that most people did not know how to access hope. I wanted to know how hope could be created, and how a plan could be put in place to deal with a deficit.

Deb started looking around the group of people at the conference, all of whom were standing in the same room with us. She pointed across the space at a gentleman on the other side.

"You need to meet Michael Lemon", she said. "He has a master's degree in hope."

I thought she was kidding, but in fact, she *was* directing me to an expert in hope. I'm no longer surprised when these alignments in the universe happen, but I certainly do enjoy them.

Michael was able to explain a few things about hope. His work builds on the work of two of his mentors, Dr. Rick Snyder and Dr. Shane Lopez, both from the University of Kansas. According to these gurus, hope is based on two beliefs:

1. **The future can be different.** This does not necessarily mean better or worse, but just the belief that things

tend to change. There is an impermanence to your situation.

2. **You can do something about it.** You are not helpless. You can build plans to move forward from wherever you find yourself.

Now, as you read these points, you may be thinking, "Yes! I have those!" Or you might be thinking, "I don't think like that at all." You may also be thinking about other people you know who either do or do not have the ability to hope.

The good news about hope is that it can be learned. If you have already learned how to be a hopeful person – great – if not, there is a path for you to develop your hope muscles. It's all rooted in what is called "Hope Theory".

Rick Snyder began developing Hope Theory back in the mid-1980s. Eventually, and after years of research, Snyder arrived at this:

> "Hope is a positive motivational state that is based on an interactively derived sense of successful (a) agency (goal-directed energy), and (b) pathways (planning to meet goals)."41

Snyder talks about the trilogy of goals, pathways and agency.

This underlines the importance of goals and goal setting in our ability to feel hopeful. Goals can be either positive (reaching for some outcome) or negative (deterring outcomes). Our goals provide targets for our thoughts and actions.

The idea of "pathways" simply means that we need to be able to find routes to attain the goals we set. We also need to be able to create alternate routes to reach our goals when our first plan runs into an obstacle.

People who Snyder considers "high-hope people" are those who, when issues arise, move effectively from one pathway to a new one, so they can reach their goals.

The term "agency thought" is the final piece in the hope puzzle and it relates to our being confident in our ability to follow our pathways.

High-hope people use self-talk like, "I can do this" and "I am not going to be stopped". This gives them mental energy to begin and follow through on their plans for reaching their goals.

In fact, high-hope people can and will take on larger, more challenging goals, and achieve them, as a direct result of this positive way of thinking. When taking on larger challenges, or when faced with increased stress in the process of attaining a goal, the high-hope person will use their abilities to work through it; thus, increasing their confidence – and their hopeful thinking. When things go wrong and goals are not achieved, the high-hope person tends to see this as useful feedback to be used in future situations.

> The confident attitude that we bring to any situation allows us to be resilient and successful on our own terms.

As a way of determining your own abilities with respect to hope, you can complete the Trait Hope Scale, shown below, which will give you a sense of where you may need to work on hope.

The Adult Trait Hope Scale[42]

Directions: Read each item carefully. Using the scale shown below, please circle the number next to each item that best describes YOU

1 Definitely False	5 Slightly True
2 Mostly False	6 Somewhat True
3 Somewhat False	7 Mostly True
4 Slightly False	8 Definitely True

1 2 3 4 5 6 7 8	1. I can think of many ways to get out of a jam
1 2 3 4 5 6 7 8	2. I energetically pursue my goals
1 2 3 4 5 6 7 8	3. I feel tired most of the time
1 2 3 4 5 6 7 8	4. There are lots of ways around any problem
1 2 3 4 5 6 7 8	5. I am easily downed in an argument
1 2 3 4 5 6 7 8	6. I can think of many ways to get the things in life that are most important to me
1 2 3 4 5 6 7 8	7. I worry about my health
1 2 3 4 5 6 7 8	8. Even when others get discouraged, I know I can find a way to solve the problem
1 2 3 4 5 6 7 8	9. My past experiences have prepared me for my future
1 2 3 4 5 6 7 8	10. I've been pretty successful in life
1 2 3 4 5 6 7 8	11. I usually find myself worrying about something
1 2 3 4 5 6 7 8	12. I meet the goals that I set for myself

Scoring information:

Pathways subscale score: Add items 1, 4, 6, and 8.
Scores on this subscale can range from 4 to 32, with higher scores indicating higher levels of pathways thinking.
Agency subscale score: Add items 2, 9, 10, and 12.
Scores on this subscale can range from 4 to 32, with higher scores indicating higher levels of agency thinking.
Total hope score: Add the pathways and Agency subscales together. Scores can range from 8 to 64, with higher scores representing higher hope levels.

Based on your results on the Adult Trait Hope Scale you can see where you have strengths and weaknesses with respect to hope. You will see your scores on:

1. **Pathways** – your ability to find ways, or routes, to reach your goals

2. **Agency** – you have the confidence to follow your pathways

3. **Total Hope Score** – the higher the score, the more you would be considered a "high-hope person".

In terms of resilience, the ability to be hopeful is key to building and remaining confident through our difficult times. It allows us to have the energy to problem solve and keep moving forward.

Fear

> "I learned that courage was not the absence of fear, but the triumph over it. The brave man is not he who does not feel afraid, but he who conquers that fear."
>
> Nelson Mandela

Managing fear is also a critical part of building confidence and resilience. We can be paralyzed by fear and will remain in terrible situations by following the old adage, "Better the devil you know." My mother refused to remove us from the household where we were being verbally and emotionally abused, for fear of "breaking up the household". George recognizes that he stayed in an unhappy marriage for a long time for fear of being single again.

Oh, and by the way, this book would have been written much sooner if not for my fear that it would be bad and no one would want to read it.

We need to have the confidence to know that we can overcome our fears. Often, we can look more reasonably at our fears and notice that our "worst case scenario" is not as bad as we think. When we think objectively about the situations we face, we can build confidence about our ability to survive them.

> "Everything you've ever wanted is on the other side of fear."
>
> George Addair

I have found that identifying what scares me allows me to find the courage to move forward through my fear. It seems that in the moment that I look carefully at the fear, I can objectively look at the *real risk* I face and consider the worst-case scenario. More often than not, this process brings me to a point where I can see that my fear is overblown. I can then see the clear path forward in a more logical and reasonable way.

This idea of looking more objectively at our world, leads us into the next factor of resilience, **Realism**.

Realism

What is Realism?

"The tendency to view or represent things as they really are."

(Dictionary.com)

This definition is simple, but accurate, with respect to what this factor entails. When we are not resilient, it can be because we are avoiding seeing things as they are. We avoid seeing the truth about our situation or our relationships, because we fear that owning this truth will force us to deal with things we would rather avoid. This can have deep and serious consequences in our lives. It can diminish our resilience and our ability to reach our goals.

How Realism Builds Resilience

We need to be constantly assessing how we are doing in our efforts to reach our goals and we must be able to identify what's getting in our way. We can't be blind to the problems and issues around us. We need to notice, when we are protecting our status quo, when it is not working for us.

Realism allows the struggles we encounter to turn into strengths and growth in the long run.

> Realism brings the necessary openness to see what's working and what's not.

When the Threat is Real

Let's face it, I'm dramatic by nature and my fears are often overblown. If I think logically, I can usually figure this out and adjust my thoughts accordingly. I did once, however, have a very different experience with "facing my fears".

After David passed, I had significant bouts of anxiety about my own health. I was deeply worried about getting sick and dying, leaving the kids on their own. I was so anxious at times that I would start to actually feel unwell. I arrived at the office of my counselor one day, ready to ask for some help with the anxiety I was feeling. I told her that I was having moments when I felt physically unwell from thinking about what would happen if I got sick and died.

I was expecting her to share some methods for managing anxious feelings, perhaps some breathing exercises? Instead she asked, "So, what would happen to the kids if you died?"

I was surprised by the question, but then shared that I thought it would be terrible for them to lose their only remaining parent. She agreed that this was a terrible, and possible, outcome. Then she suggested that rather than beating myself up about worrying about this outcome, I should recognize it as a reasonable thing to be afraid of and give myself a hug when I found myself worrying about it.

From that point on, if I thought about dying and leaving my kids alone, I would say to myself, "that would be really bad", and then I would move on. I never felt the physical signs of my worries again. Identifying the fear, even when it is not overblown, helps me remain grounded and resilient.

So, the point is that sometimes you are afraid of something that is truly scary. And that's okay. You should be afraid of those things. Don't assume that all fears can be overcome or that you should be working to stop being fearful of all things.

Sometimes, facing your fear means recognizing that there is a real and true risk, and you are quite right in noticing it. This clarity will help you to consider this fear more rationally or realistically, plan for contingencies, and not allow it to have more power than it should.

Seeing the Whole Picture

The obvious example of realism shows up in David's story. He was the king of realism. Some people loved this about him, some could not handle hearing his frank observations. Either way, he did not hang onto the status quo when it was not working.

It was just several hours after being diagnosed with stage four colon cancer that I found him sitting up in bed, smiling, and waiting for our family doctor to come and tell him about our next steps. I was thinking that our next steps would be crying and screaming and asking, "Why us?" David had moved on.

Through his resilience he showed exactly how realism can be used to make sure that you don't make more of your problems than you need to. Of course, his cancer was terrible and his prognosis was never good, but it was only part of his story. Cancer did not define him. It only impacted how he spent some of his time and efforts during his last three years of life.

Think of it this way: David was a cancer patient, but he was also a father, husband, brother, hockey coach, business manager, and farmer. In many ways, he just added cancer treatments to his to-do list. It became part of his life. He left chemo and went to the hockey rink, often with the slow-drip chemo bottle attached to his side. He took his "ostomy bag", a knapsack with supplies, and a change of clothes, with him everywhere he went. He joked that it was no different than when we used to carry a diaper bag everywhere. It was just part of his gear.

> He did not define himself as a cancer patient, but rather he was a husband, father, and friend with cancer.

Realism means seeing things as they are. It means not ignoring the facts of the situation. In some cases, that means that you need to own your issues and problems and not avoid them. In other cases, it means that you need to "right size" your problems and allow yourself to start to see them as fixable.

In most cases, our problems don't define us. They are just part of our journey.

Sinisa's Story

My friend Sinisa exemplifies what it means to live a life grounded in realism.

His life has involved adjusting to difficult and changing realities, and managing through with resilience. Imagine you are one day a star soccer player, the next day handed a gun and told to kill your friends. Your focus is now on staying alive, and soccer dreams seem a world away. Sinisa's family as a whole, in fact, has shown incredible resilience in their ability to move forward after experiencing struggles most of us cannot fathom.

In the case of his father, imagine you are one day a successful banker, and after surviving a war and escaping with your family, you are only qualified to wash dishes in a Chinese restaurant. You don't even speak the language of your new country. No one you meet at work has any idea that you were smart, articulate, and successful in your past life. You are still a smart person, but you no longer have the prestige and respected position you once had. What would you do?

Sinisa's story takes us to a horrendous moment in history, to a city under siege, to the former Yugoslavia. After Slovenia and Croatia seceded Yugoslavia in 1991, the Socialist Republic of Bosnia and Herzegovina passed a referendum for independence, intending also to leave. The political representatives of the Bosnian Serbs rejected the claim for independence, and the war began. Between 1992 and 1996, one hundred thousand people were killed, and 2.2 million were displaced.

During the war, Sinisa and his family were in Sarajevo, the capital city of Bosnia and Herzegovina. Between April 5, 1992 and February 29, 1996, a total of 1,425 days, this city was under siege. Sinisa was, literally, in the middle of it. He was physically in the middle of a city under attack and he was a young man of fighting age, and expected to fight.

He spent his time avoiding the army representatives, who combed the streets looking for able-bodied young men. When they found you, they would hand you a gun and send you to the front lines.

For Sinisa and many of his peers, the war was not something they felt was theirs to fight. They had friends on both sides of the political lines and had no wish to kill their friends. But young men of fighting age were being rounded up and told to fight.

With the war happening right in the city where he lived, moving in and out of the fighting could be done by hiding out with friends and family. Sinisa would move around day to day, staying in different places, in order to avoid being found and sent to fight again. He was not always successful in staying hidden. To this day, he does not share much about what happened to him on those streets.

It's hard to imagine living under these circumstances. It's not hard to imagine that this experience would leave indelible scars. So, looking at Sinisa today, it's amazing to see the life he has built and the way he sees the world.

In 1995, Sinisa and his family came to Canada. They settled in Kitchener, Ontario and started to build a life. Sinisa had survived a lifetime worth of trauma, but he was only 19 years old. His little brother, who had been sent out of the country during the war, was seventeen.

Sinisa's dad, the banker, found work washing dishes; eventually securing a better job in a factory. He worked there until his retirement, fifteen years later. Remember, this man was a highly successful business leader in his homeland.

Sinisa's mom is also an example of the resilience we see in this family. She was a highly educated musician who came to Canada and began sharing her love of music with students. By the time she retired, she had taught music for fifty years.

The family is now well established in Canada. Sinisa has two children; Ana, who is super smart and thinks and acts in many ways like her dad, and Marko, who shares his dad's love of soccer. They are both great kids as a result of the example set by their parents. Their mom, Danijela, an interior designer, is originally from Yugoslavia and knows well the experience of war. They are surrounded by a strong community of Serbians.

Sinisa has a good job and a beautiful family. He also has a side business; training soccer players. He has seen significant success with developing athletes who have been recruited by top teams. His soccer addiction leads him to share openly his love of the sport with anyone who wants to play. While teaching soccer, he feels he is sharing his special talent with the world. I'm not sure he realizes that he is teaching things that go far beyond the sport of soccer, such as leadership, respect for others, and how to live a contented, authentic life. He is respected by everyone he works with, and in all areas of his life.

When you talk to Sinisa, you get no sense of regret, no sense of the trauma he has survived. Instead, you feel uplifted by his positive attitude, his gratitude for what he has and the life he enjoys today, and his constant concern for others.

According to Sinisa:

> "My job is to be the wind at the backs of all these people, my soccer players, my co-workers, and my family. It's important to think and wish good about everybody and everything. Not just to say it, but to really mean it. And whenever I find myself in a bad situation, I always say to myself, "I've seen worse

than this in my life and I will get out of
this, too."

Beyond this basic sense of courage, Sinisa has a few
other strategies for getting through tough times.

When he reflects on his recovery after the war, he
credits his parents for setting an example for him and his
brother to follow. They showed the boys that carrying on by
looking forward was the best way to get over the past. They
also set high expectations for the boys to succeed in their
new home.

I'm guessing that when you see your parents moving
forward in a positive and determined way, you don't consider
feeling sorry for yourself or looking for excuses as to why
you can't move forward. You carry on because it is the only
way to make sense of the situation. You must make a new
life, in part to make up for what is lost. If you don't, then
the loss is for nothing.

> I see realism in this story. It is in
> this understanding that the past is
> over and the future is full of hope.

When you talk to Sinisa, you quickly get a strong
sense of his values. He is unwilling to compromise these
values, as they are long learned from his parents and are an
important part of the man he is today. He has values around
gratitude for what you have, helping others without the
expectation of repayment, and following your passions, so
that you can share them with the world. These values explain
how he has successfully built a life after all that trauma. They
also explain how the rest of his family has done the same.
Values like gratitude and helping and using your talents lead
you forward and propel you through your struggles.

245

> There are many more examples of people who have survived war, escape, and rebuilding a life. Many have done so with great success. They seem strengthened in their resolve and determined to make their lives meaningful.

Sinisa has witnessed that in his community, some have fared well, and others have struggled more. He feels that the difference depends on the ability to put the past behind you and move forward. You can't blame them, but this is the difference between being resilient, and not.

In Sinisa's experience, the difference comes in part from dwelling on the trauma, unable to see what is positive around you. You must have the ability to find an outlet for your emotional injuries and not allow them to interfere with your attitude and outlook. If you can't, the war stays with you and keeps you from finding peace within yourself.

> "Success is not final, failure is not fatal: it is the courage to continue that counts."
>
> Winston Churchill

Now, let's be clear, we are just beginning to understand the psychological injuries people endure and how it impacts them. We know that Post Traumatic Stress Disorder is complicated and difficult to understand and treat. I don't want to pretend that Sinisa holds all the answers to surviving and thriving after living through war, only that he is an example of someone who demonstrates resilience despite his horrendous experience.

A Realistic Process

> "When I argue with reality, I lose—but only 100 percent of the time."
>
> Byron Katie

We build resilience by noticing what works and what does not. Whether you are trying to change your emotional state or working toward a specific career or life goal, you need to figure out how things are going, so you can adjust your course accordingly.

We need to be able to look objectively at our situation and see what is happening. We need to collect the data to decide what changes to make. There are several ways to do this.

Here is a simple process that will allow you to gain the insights you need to be a "realist".

First, look back at the plans you have made. If you wrote specific goals and action plans, how are you doing so far? What is left undone or is behind schedule?

Take note of these things. They are your focus areas.

Now, consider each focus area. Think and write some notes about:

1. What have you tried?

2. What have you learned so far?

3. What is working well?

4. What is not working?

By analyzing your answers, you can get some specific ideas about what you need to change. Try to remain non-judgmental in this process, as you will be better able to pull out the true issues. This process allows you to get objective feedback and you may find some surprising results. You may notice your assumptions in a way you might not have previously. You will recognize things that are getting in your way that you had not noticed before. You will certainly see what your next steps need to be.

This kind of analysis will sharpen your ability to view things with realism, and will lead to significant changes in how you approach people, situations, and your path forward. This is the path to resilience.

Find Trusted Advisors

Another great way to gather information and ideas about your situation is to ask for feedback from those around you. You either have, or should find, people who can give their opinions or observations that may help you see things you might be missing.

My husband George, for instance, will notice immediately if I am short on patience in dealing with the kids. In my less resilient moments, I just get angry with him for providing the feedback in a "shoot the messenger" fashion. If I'm open to his feedback, I can usually figure out what is going on and make adjustments to my behavior.

Of course, not everyone you know will fall into the category of "trusted advisor", nor should they. Find people you admire or trust who will provide feedback with your best interests in mind. Listen with an open mind and an interest in learning, but remember that the opinions you hear are simply the perceptions of that person. The data may or may not be valid, that's up to you to decide.

Watch Your Values

Sometimes realism involves noticing what's not working and re-examining your values to see if they need to be adjusted.

At times we are doing things that are in line with what is important to us, but in the end, we are not getting what we expect.

My friend Sinisa has a great example of this. He is such a wonderful, humble man. He never tells anyone about his own successes, only the successes of his team, or those around him.

When I lobbied to have him included in the book, *The Leadership Challenge*, I was merely responding to a request from the authors for examples of great leaders. Sinisa was an obvious choice. I wrote about Sinisa, it was edited, and included in the book in a section called "Show Concern for Others" and remains there two editions later. He's just that good.

And yet, Sinisa tells no one about his talents and accomplishments. Here is what he is noticing now:

> "Sometimes we need to be aware of our qualities and maybe advertise them more. I grew up in the world where you need to be good and quiet, and eventually someone will recognize this. Once recognized, you'll be placed in the position where your full capacity will

come to light. In the western world, it is normal to advertise yourself, but I found many situations where people who speak so highly of themselves are nowhere near the competence they should be. I think I should have more self-awareness of my qualities."

So, Sinisa has strong values around being humble, working hard, and helping other people. He has always assumed that by following these values, success would just follow. And don't get me wrong, he has been successful, just not as successful as he deserves to be. He has done a great job, and the people around him have benefited from his efforts. But he needs to learn that his humble nature is actually getting in the way of greater success. And in the long run, he is missing out on opportunities where he could help even more. It's not just his own loss, but a loss to those around him who would benefit from his leadership.

Luckily, he is realizing this now, with still many years ahead in his career and life, and he can adjust his sails and begin to make sure people know the strengths and talents he brings to the table.

Learning Focus

"Nothing changes if nothing changes, and if I keep doing what I've always done, I'll keep getting what I've always got, and will keep feeling what I always felt."

Earnie Larson, Addiction Author & Counsellor

What is Learning Focus?

As it relates to resilience, having a **Learning Focus** means that you can and will modify your behaviour based on your experience. You don't just know what is working and not working, but you actively train yourself to do more of the behaviours that are working and modify those that are not. You are not stuck in old habits that are getting in your way. You have the tenacity to stick to the new habits that are serving you well. **Learning Focus** is about turning the data you gather through **Self-Awareness** and **Realism** into action and personal growth.

How Learning Builds Resilience

Earnie Larsen died in 2011, but he leaves us with the above quote, born out of experience and difficulty. He was a pioneer in the field of recovery from addictive behaviors and an author and lecturer on the topic of addiction. He had also been a counselor for more than forty years.

In Earnie's words we hear the essence of the factor **Learning Focus**. If we want to improve our situation and be happier, more content or more successful, we need to make a change. And we are much more in control of these changes than we often realize. We can change our situation or we can change how we respond to it. This is **Learning Focus**.

We need to be able to make changes to our behaviour in order to achieve real change in our lives. We need to put a plan in place to create the change we want. Then, we need to implement that plan to bring about the positive outcomes we seek.

Ever Tried to Lose Weight?

A simple but common example of learning focus happens to most of us if and when we try to lose weight. You may have joined a weight loss "club" or found a diet book or fad. You learn how to change your habits, and before you know it, you are losing weight.

For David and I, our weight loss program was amazing. We learned how to manage what we were eating in ways that we could make work. We learned how to substitute some foods for others that contained fewer calories. We learned about portion control.

In six months, I lost fifty-five pounds. In a year, David lost 200 pounds! And he kept it off by continuing to use the new habits and behaviors. Again, he was resilient to the core and his ability to learn what was working and what was not is another example of this resilience.

I have heard people comment on how he first lost all that weight, and then he got sick, as if the weight loss was a waste of effort. I always think that it was wonderful that he lost all that weight before he got sick, as I'm quite sure his cancer journey, including surgery and chemotherapy, would have been more problematic with all that extra weight.

In any event, David was able to keep his weight off by sticking to his new habits. Many of us lose weight only to gain it back as our old habits creep back in. This is the challenge of **Learning Focus.**

How to Change Habits

Many of us are not as good at changing our habits or maintaining those changes.

I, for one, tend to fall back into my old habits quite easily when it comes to food. When I'm stressed, I tend to eat the very things that I know I should not, and I end up feeling more stressed about how I have just eaten that whole row of cookies. I do find that if I can get some momentum with a new habit, I'm much more likely to stick to it.

I also find that I'm much more likely to change a habit or acquire a new one if I'm kind to myself. If I treat myself with compassion, I'm more likely to be successful with the change.

> The more I beat myself up about a less than ideal habit, the less energy I have, to change it.

Part of **Learning Focus** involves giving some thought to why we are so attached to the unhealthy or bad habit. If I can notice why that habit formed in the first place, I can move toward a better understanding of how to change it.

For me, a great example is my habit of snapping at my family when I am stressed or upset. This is a habit that is strongly entrenched both in my personality style (controlling and reactive) and my upbringing (my father was also quick to anger). When I catch myself reacting in a way I don't like, I can at least understand why this happens. Then I can think of the behavior as changeable and recognize that *I am not my habits*, they are just my most common ways of behaving.

Again, I try to be compassionate with myself rather than beat myself up. My habits are not part of me; although, they certainly feel like they are – and I can change them if I am willing to do the hard work. This is not easy, but it's better than not attempting to change because I feel that my efforts will be futile.

Without these changes I am destined to repeat the old habits and will be unable to reach my goals.

How to Change Unhealthy Habits

According to Teri Goetz, in her article for *Psychology Today*, there are ten steps to changing unhealthy habits:[43]

1. **Identify the habits you want to change**. This means bringing what is usually unconscious (or at least ignored) to your awareness. It does not mean beating yourself up about it. Make a list of things you'd like to change, and then, pick one.

2. **Look at what you are getting out of it**. In other words, how is your habit serving you? Are you looking for comfort in food? Numbness in wine? An outlet or connection online? Stress

alleviation through eating or nail biting? This doesn't have to be a long, complex process. You'll figure it out— and you'll have some good ideas about how to switch it up for healthier outcomes.

3. **Honor your own wisdom.** Here's a common scenario: you feel like you have no downtime, so you stay up way too late binge-watching your favorite show. You know you'll be exhausted and less productive the next day, but you feel "entitled" to do something fun, just for you. Your wisdom knows this is not a healthy way to solve your problem. Use that wisdom to build something into your schedule that will provide what you really want. Realize you do have the answers and are capable of doing something different.

4. **Choose something to replace the unhealthy habit.** Just willing yourself to change isn't enough, because it does not address the underlying benefit of the behavior you want to replace. What can you do instead of standing in front of the fridge when you're stressed? If you have a plan, you are "armed" with tools and a replacement behavior. Next time you catch yourself standing in front of the refrigerator and not hungry, use the tools and try a replacement behavior.

Some ideas: breathe into the count of 4 and breathe out to the count of 8, focusing only on your breathing. Do that 4 times and see how you feel. If you need more support, stand there until you come up with one reason why you shouldn't continue with this habit. *This is a key step. When you do something different to replace an unhealthy habit, acknowledge to yourself that you are doing it differently.* You need to bring whatever it is that is subconscious to the conscious mind, so you can emphasize your ability to change. It can be as simple as saying to yourself, "Look at that. I made a better choice."

5. **Remove triggers.** If Doritos are a trigger, throw them out on a day you feel strong enough to do so. If you crave a cigarette when you drink socially, avoid social triggers— restaurants, bars, nights out with friends ... just for a while... until you feel secure in your new habit. Sometimes, certain people are our triggers. Remember that you end up being like the five people you hang out with most. Look at who those people are: do they inspire you or drag you down?

6. **Visualize yourself changing**. Serious visualization retrains your brain, and you want to think differently about your ability to change—so, spend some time every day envisioning yourself with new habits. Exercising and enjoying it, eating healthy foods, fitting into those jeans. See yourself engaged in happy conversation with someone,

instead of standing in the back of the room. This kind of visualization really works. The now-familiar idea that "nerves that fire together wire together" is based on the idea that the more you think about something and do it, the more it becomes wired in your brain, and your default choice can actually be a healthier one for you.

7. **Monitor your negative self-talk.** The refrain in your brain can seriously affect your default behaviors. So, when you catch yourself saying, "I'm fat" or "No one likes me" reframe it or redirect it. Reframing is like rewriting the script. Replace it with, "I'm getting healthy" or "My confidence is growing." Redirecting is when you add to your negative self-talk, such as, "I'm fat – but I'm working my way into a healthier lifestyle." Judging yourself only keeps you stuck. So, reframe, redirect, and retrain.

8. **Take baby steps, if necessary**. Even if you can't follow through 100% with a new habit, try to do it in part. For example, if you've blocked an hour to exercise and you have a doctor's appointment during that hour, find another time to squeeze in at least 15 minutes of exercise that day. This reinforces, retrains your mind that "this is my new habit."

9. **Accept that you will sometimes falter.** We all do. Habits don't change overnight. Remember that habits are

simply routines we've developed so we don't have to remind ourselves to do them – like brushing your teeth. Love yourself any time you miss or mess up your new routine-building, then carry on with a smile.

10. **Know that it will take time.** Give yourself several weeks to a few months to create a change in a habit. That bundle of nerves in your brain needs time to change your default settings and reinforce the new ones.

These steps are great advice we can use when we are tackling those difficult habits. Teri focuses on health-related habits, but I think these guides would work for any habits. I have tried these ideas with respect to my "hot-headedness" and it really helps… most of the time.

> Changing habits is not easy but being able to make these changes is key to our resilience.

Immunity to Change

In my experience, some of the changes we need to make are deeper than the habits we might be able to tackle with a ten-step process. Some are rooted deeply in our emotions and our ways of thinking and behaving, and require a stronger tool.

> "You leave old habits behind by starting out with the thought, 'I release the need for this in my life.'"

Wayne Dyer

A model called "Immunity to Change" can help us understand what is stopping us from sticking to new habits. This model, and the book by the same name, was developed at the Harvard Graduate School of Education by Robert Kegan and Lisa Lahey.[44]

The model teaches us that when trying to make change in our lives, we often have "one foot on the gas, the other on the brake." This conflicting situation is hard to fix because the factors operating the brake are largely unconscious.

An example many of us are familiar with would be our health goals. Whether we want to lose weight, exercise more, eat healthier, or a combination of those things, we know we can be our own worst enemies in our efforts to reach our goals. We know how to get there, but we sabotage ourselves.

Kegan and Lahey point to research that shows that when heart doctors tell their seriously ill patients to change their diet, exercise more, stop smoking and reduce stress, only one in seven patients will make these changes. That means that the other six, despite presumably wanting to continue living, were unable to make the relatively straight-forward changes necessary.

It seems impossible; yet we know from experience that there is often a significant gap between our genuine intentions and what we are actually able to bring about in our lives. We are getting in our own way.

In the case of heart patients, they may fear things like "being seen as weak or sick" or "getting old". These deep fears interfere with their ability to change their habits, despite the fact that they may [dramatically shorten their life span] die as a result of not changing those habits. We all fall prey to self-sabotage to some degree. Fortunately, there is a process we can follow to help us overcome such issues.

Try this:

Step 1: Think about a goal you have set for yourself, but have not achieved, or a commitment to yourself you have not kept.

Step 2: Now list all the things you are doing AND not doing that are keeping you from achieving that goal. These are known as obstructive behaviors.

Step 3: Now, do an honest self-inventory. Make a list of the reasons why you are doing the things you listed in step two. You may find that you have uncovered the worries or fears keeping you from doing what you wanted to do (your goal).

When you go through these steps, you will have a list you can work with. Take a look at what you wrote down in Step 3. These are your true commitments. You are committed to these things more than you are committed to your goals. This is why you are not accomplishing your goals.

If I run my challenge of "maintaining a healthy weight" through this process, I recognize that instead of doing all the healthy things I know how to do, I tend to do these obstructive behaviors:

- Use food as comfort when I'm bored or stressed

- Eat the foods I love rather than the ones that are good for me

Once I start to eat things I shouldn't, I'll continue to eat them for the rest of the day with the attitude of: "well, I've blown it now, anyway".

When I look at this list it seems so stupid. But, it's true. I often get to the end of the day and I can't believe that I blew it again.

Okay, that's Step Two out of the way, now how about Step Three? If I think about the reasons why I do these things I come up with:

- I am committed to not being bored

- I am committed to enjoying the foods I love (not the healthy ones!)

- I am committed to procrastinating my weight loss goals and putting off the hard work until "tomorrow"

- I think that if no one sees me eating poorly, they won't ever know and be disappointed with me.

This second list is very interesting. It feels raw and personal. I don't want anyone to see it. That's how it will probably feel for you when you try this process. You are uncovering the things that are getting in your way, the things you are not even aware are driving you forward.

My list seems silly. It makes me wonder why an intelligent, mature woman could be this illogical. I now need to find some compassion for myself and start thinking of strategies that will deal with the items from Step Three. That is the only way to really make the change happen. It's not easy, and it's certainly not going to go perfectly, but at least now I'm focused on the right things and have the chance to make real change.

As Kegan and Lahey have shown in *The Immunity to Change*, it's not because we don't have good intentions that we don't accomplish our goals. We need to figure out how we are getting in our own way and fix the problem of our worries, fears and assumptions.

> The more we practice, the better we get, and the more resilient we will be.

We need to courageously tackle our challenges, knowing that we can do it. We need to be hopeful and assume that no matter how bad things may seem, they will not remain that way. We need to look objectively at our situations, relationships and habits, and figure out what is working, what is not, and what needs to be done to improve.

> Even when things are moving forward, we want to be looking realistically at what could be better and how to improve.

Finally, we need to implement the plans we make by changing habitual behaviors when necessary. We need to stop doing the things that are not working for us, and start doing things that will move us forward.

The new habits we establish are key to our resilience. They are the path forward toward our life goals. In this way, we move from excuses to success, on our own terms.

DYNAMIC THINKING

Confidence · Realism · Learning Focus

In this chapter we talked about:

Confidence

Keeping a Positive Attitude – you need to look for the good in situations and not get bogged down by the problems or risks

A Leap of Faith – you won't always be sure something will work, but you have to jump in and give it a try

Hope – you need to believe that difficult situations will not stay that way forever and you can work through struggles knowing there will be a better future

Fear – managing fear so that you can build the confidence to take on your struggles is key to resilience

Realism

When the Threat is Real – recognize that sometimes things that scare you are truly scary

Seeing the Whole Picture – don't make more of your problems than you need to

A Realistic Process – you can assess what is working and what is not

Find Trusted Advisors – others can help you see things more clearly. Go find these people

Watch Your Values – sometimes your prior learning teaches you to follow values that no longer make sense

Learning Focus

How to Change Habits – there is a stair-step way to tackle changing your habits

Immunity to Change – when changing habits proves difficult, this model will help you look at the underlying issues that are keeping you from success

For more information please visit:
www.theresilienceway.com

Chapter Nine

Physical Health

PHYSICAL HEALTH

Sleep · Nutrition · Exercise

> "It is health that is real wealth and not pieces of gold and silver."
>
> Mahatma Gandhi

The final Element of Resilience is **Physical Health**.

As anyone who has been seriously ill can attest, if you don't have your health, you have nothing. Although this statement is simplistic, it is basically true. As resilient people, we need to maintain our physical health in order to be able to play in the other areas of resilience.

> In order to achieve our personal goals, we need to be healthy.

This Element involves three Factors: **Sleep, Nutrition** and **Exercise.**

If you don't **Sleep** well you know how important this Factor is to your health and well-being. To the extent that we can we need to develop good sleep habits and get the rest we need.

Nutrition is also critical. For many of us this means using knowledge and information we already have to follow good and healthy eating habits.

267

Exercise is key to living well and maintaining good health. There are many benefits to exercise that we can take advantage of if we make it a regular part of our lives.

Don't Ignore Your Health

Many people can share a story about a time when they or their loved ones did not go early enough to the doctor, even when they knew something was wrong.

I lost a good friend to breast cancer twenty years ago because she was afraid to go see her doctor. By the time she got there, it was no longer a treatable case. It is not uncommon to be fearful of going to see a medical professional. We often put off these visits for no good reason, until the situation becomes critical. Ever waited on a tooth ache until it was absolutely intolerable? It may well have been an easy treatment when it first started to hurt, but by the time it is really sore it will be a much more difficult fix.

> This tendency to avoid looking after our health is quite common, but it is certainly not resilient.

David's case, caught early enough, would have been curable. Colon cancer found early, while only in the colon, is often curable. If you are putting off booking a scope because it seems like an uncomfortable experience, I'd suggest you consider the discomfort of surgery and chemotherapy, not to mention the colostomy bag. Unfortunately, in David's case, by the time there were symptoms, it was too late. He was only forty-two when he was diagnosed and that's just too young for anyone to think about testing for colon cancer, until his colon was blocked by the tumor, and by then it was also on his liver. I hope his case is a warning for others though, and that we will all get simple tests done to avoid finding ourselves in the same situation as David.

We are resilient when we take care of ourselves.

We don't always get to control our physical health, and again, many can tell stories about how their health became an enormous struggle. But even in these times, we want to separate out what we can control from what we can't, and then work on maintaining and improving our physical health as best we can. We do this through good habits in the areas of **sleep, nutrition, and exercise.**

If you don't generally sleep well, then you don't need to be told that this is an important factor. Sleep is critical to our health. It is our time to replenish and heal our body and mind. When you sleep well and wake rested, you are ready to take on the challenges of life. You are much better able to deal with adversity. This is the power of **Sleep**.

In the discussion of this factor, we will look at how to develop good sleep habits and a bit more about the benefits of great sleeping.

Nutrition is key to your health. You need to ensure that you are giving your body what it needs to be healthy and energetic. For many of us, our issues are not with a lack of nutritional information or understanding, but with our abilities to manage our eating habits.

You need to be knowledgeable about current nutritional recommendations and be able to adapt your eating habits accordingly. Some people find following healthy eating guidelines easy, like my tall, lanky husband, George, and they enjoy the benefits of good nutrition.

If I hear George say one more time, "I'm fifty now, so I can't eat things that are not good for me…" I'm going to slug him!

Some of us, myself included, need to watch our habits when it comes to our eating and make sure we are taking care to eat the right things, in the right quantities. We see a bag of cookies and think, "Just one won't hurt me", only to devour the entire bag. (Once you pass the half-way point you just have to finish them up and destroy the evidence, right?) In any event, we need to know what we should be eating and we need to align our habits to this knowledge, so that we can be both healthy and resilient.

> It seems that we are likely to live longer than our ancestors, but will we be as active and healthy at the end of our lives as they were?

If you live to be 100, but have been confined to a wheelchair for twenty of those years, are you going to enjoy your life? You need to keep your body active and able, and in order to do this you need to **Exercise**.

I struggle to do this with consistency, but I know it is critical. I think about how able my Mom is, and although I can't tell you how old she is, no one thinks she is as old as her birth certificate says she is. She is busy and active and enjoys the benefits of having been an active person her whole life. That's resilient.

Sleep

How Sleep Builds Resilience

Having restful sleep is an important part of maintaining our physical and mental health. The links, in fact, to mental health are now being better understood and research in this area is showing that quality sleep is a key factor in our mental wellness. Once again, the resilience elements link together and improving in one area supports your overall resilience.

A Good Night's Sleep

Many people struggle with getting a good night's sleep. When they are struggling with issues in their lives, they sleep even less and/or with poorer quality. We must not measure our sleeping success in quantity alone. More sleep is not necessarily better.

The amount of sleep that most of us get has actually decreased over the past several decades.[45] There is even evidence that we are sleeping 25% less than folks did 100 years ago. This does not necessarily mean we are worse off though, from a resilience point of view.

In fact, the amount of sleep you get might differ considerably from the amount someone else requires. Sleep quantity varies from one individual to another. You need to figure out what works for you, and then make sure you are getting sufficient, high-quality hours of shut-eye.

In order to improve your sleep, consider your "sleep hygiene" including:

- Watch your caffeine intake, especially as you approach bedtime. Caffeine stimulates the central nervous system, increases your heart rate and adrenaline production, and suppresses melatonin production (a key sleep-promoting substance).[46]

- Alcohol can be a problem, too, as it interferes with sleep quality during the second half of the night. It is also a diuretic, so you may find yourself getting up to use the bathroom in the middle of the night.

- Your eating habits may also affect your sleep. Eating foods with refined sugars before bed might make it harder to sleep. Eating a large amount may also interfere with your sleep while your body tries to digest your meal. A snack before bed, especially one including rice, oats and/or dairy (all of which increase melatonin levels) can help you sleep.

- Exercise will help you sleep, but the timing of it can be important. Exercise increases adrenaline production, so for many people, exercising right before bed will interfere with their sleep. This also depends on the type and intensity of the exercise.

The strategies that will increase the quality of sleep will vary considerably from person to person. In addition to the items from the sleep research, I would suggest the following from my own experience:

- Separate your sleep space from the space you use when you work or watch your favorite shows. You may find that the TV helps you get to sleep, but make sure it is not encouraging you to watch more than you would otherwise. If you stay up later because you get caught up binge watching your favorite show, that's not helping. Personally, I have banned the TV from my bedroom.

- Create a routine so that your body knows it is time for sleep. This might involve a bath or a cup of tea as part of your transition to sleep. You might also try self-talk by announcing out loud that "it's bedtime and I'm going to sleep well and feel great tomorrow" as a way of signalling for your brain to switch gears. If yoga or stretching is relaxing for you, try some before bed.

- Pay attention to what is keeping you awake and think about what you could do to alleviate these elements. Some will be outside of your control but, guaranteed, some are not.

  Are you fussing about a conversation you need to have with a co-worker or family member about something stressful? Or are you debating whether to deal with it at all? Accept that you can't do anything about it until morning and refuse to give up any more sleep over it. Perhaps your "To Do" list is keeping you awake? Try keeping a notepad or a recording device next to your bed for quick notes, and then you can go to sleep, knowing you will resolve them in the morning.

- Practice basic meditation techniques to help settle your mind for the night. Try to add thoughts that are more restful, including relaxing and repetitive visualizations (like canoeing down a quiet stream or walking on a forest path).

- Try napping. Perhaps short, afternoon naps will help with your overall restfulness. Not everyone can nap, but for some of us, this is a great way to unwind and be ready for the rest of the day.

- If you have tried the basics and still are not sleeping well, ask your doctor for help.

Don't Fall into Bad Sleeping Habits

People slide into bad sleeping habits without realizing what they are doing. Here are a couple of common situations I have heard about…

Musical Beds

Friends had a toddler who began waking in the night and whining to come into bed with them. They let her in, rather than deal with the conflict and sleep loss involved in getting her to return to her own bed. No surprise, this became standard practice, and the child began to arrive every night. The wife found it hard to sleep in the now-crowded bed, so she moved each night to the guest room.

Fast forward several years and now there are three children and no extra beds. Now the children and parents all play "musical beds" as they try to find a good spot to sleep. Everyone's sleep is disturbed, either by a child looking for better digs, or in the case of the children, by the habits they have developed of waking in the night and searching for beds.

This friend now has a teenage daughter who has trouble sleeping. Had they just settled the first child back into bed each night in the first place, they would all be sleeping better. Instead, they have all developed poor sleeping habits.

Now, if you are thinking, "But my little one could not be stopped and would just keep coming back." remember that I have four children and I know what it's like to return a child to bed for the eighth time in one night. But you won't be doing that forever, and in the long run you will lose less sleep than if you give in and agree to live a sleep-disturbed life until they go to college. You aren't doing your child any favors either, as you are training them to have poor sleep habits.

A caveat... I'm not passing any judgment here regarding folks who choose to sleep with their children in a "family bed" arrangement. Although that would not be my choice, it is exactly that, a choice. The friends I'm referring to wanted everyone to sleep in their own beds, which is why they provided separate bedrooms for each child in the first place.

What's with the Snoring?

I grew up with a father who snored like a lumberjack or a lumberjack's buzz saw. His snoring was, I'm sure, made worse by his drinking and overeating. In any event, I am now trained to sleep through just about any noise. Lucky me.

However, I know so many people whose sleep is constantly disturbed by their spouse's snoring. Just like the folks with toddlers in their beds, they end up moving around the house through the night, trying to find a quiet spot.

I am surprised though when I hear stories like this, because I wonder why people don't make this issue a priority and find a fix. There are multiple snoring fixes, and in most of the cases I see, none of these options have been tried. If your snoring is affecting others, go see your doctor. You may have a medical condition, such as sleep apnea, which is entirely treatable. Why on earth would you not want to find a way to sleep better? Why not stop disturbing your partner's sleep?

A Chance to Dream

Different from Shakespeare's quote in Hamlet, "perchance to dream", where Hamlet is afraid of the dreams that will come when he dies, I absolutely love to dream. It is in my dreams that I sort out the day's many bits and pieces. In my dreams, I visit with loved ones who have passed. In some dreams, I am still married to David and I awake feeling like I had time with him. He is often healthy in my dreams and this is a special treat. Every once in a while, he is sick and dying in my dreams and I awake reminded of the trauma we went through. That's not my favorite, but it does allow me to notice and not forget how difficult our journey has been (the kids and I) and how resilient we really are. In some dreams both George and David are present and it's as if that's perfectly normal. When I wake up, I am reminded that our situation is actually perfectly normal in the grand sense. It is as it should be. There is no conflict.

So, as I wake from a good sleep, I am gifted with dreams to notice, process and from which to create meaning. I pay close attention to my thoughts as I wake up, as these are the purest thoughts of my day. There is often wisdom in these thoughts. They are sent from the special combination of my dreams and my waking mind. They help me ground myself in the new day.

I love this poem by the wonderful poet, David Whyte.

What to Remember When Waking

In that first hardly noticed moment in which you wake,
coming back to this life from the other
more secret, moveable and frighteningly honest world
where everything began,
there is a small opening into the new day
which closes the moment you begin your plans.

What you can plan is too small for you to live.
What you can live wholeheartedly will make plans enough
for the vitality hidden in your sleep.

To be human is to become visible
while carrying what is hidden as a gift to others.
To remember the other world in this world
is to live in your true inheritance.

You are not a troubled guest on this earth,
you are not an accident amidst other accidents
you were invited from another and greater night

than the one from which you have just emerged.

Now, looking through the slanting light of the morning
window
toward the mountain presence of everything that can be
what urgency calls you to your one love?
What shape waits in the seed of you
to grow and spread its branches
against a future sky?

Is it waiting in the fertile sea?
In the trees beyond the house?
In the life you can imagine for yourself?
In the open and lovely white page on the writing desk?

Cherish your sleep. Know that it is so important to your ability to be the person you want to be. Work on it. Deal with the issues that interfere with you getting the rest you need. Your mind and your body need proper sleep.

Nutrition

How Nutrition Builds Resilience

Many people do a great job of eating well. Some of us do not, or could be doing better. For many, a lack of information is not the issue. It can be more about our emotional health than we might like to admit.

When we are under the stress of life's difficult times, it is even harder to maintain good eating habits. So, we need to:

- Understand the basics of nutrition. This includes the basic recommendations for total caloric intake and the benefits and pitfalls of fats, sugar, and food additives. We need to know if we are getting all the nutrients, including vitamins and minerals, that our bodies need.

- Notice our food tendencies. This includes any emotional eating habits we have developed and finding strategies to overcome these issues.

- Avoid fad diets and quick fixes for weight/food issues. These tend to be short term plans and can even be unhealthy as they stress your body and create "yo-yo" weight losses and gains. With these suspect 'nutrition' plans, you can end up heavier, less healthy, and feeling unsuccessful, which does not encourage good food habits, or resilience in general.

If the first two steps cannot be done on our own, we need to seek professional help from a doctor or nutritionist so we can address our issues safely and successfully.

Sometimes I feel like good nutrition is a moving target. I find that the media and my social circles are full of advice on the latest and greatest nutrition options. At times, it seems like it is constantly changing. Nevertheless, I try to figure out what makes sense for me and my family, and I adjust our eating accordingly.

Many years ago, one of these adjustments meant removing fat from our diet. That was interesting, because David and I both gained considerable weight on our low-fat diet.

That was not working.

Since then, I have realized that carbs are an issue. It is really difficult to manage your caloric intake if bread and pasta are a major part of your diet. Lately, I have been learning more about the effects of sugar on my nutrition. There is growing evidence that many of us need to manage our sugar intake. When I hear someone describe the way sugar reacts in our bodies, and the concept of "sugar addiction", I can picture myself running to the kitchen to find something sweet. And I usually do!

Let's be clear... I am NOT a nutritionist. I do not make recommendations regarding nutrition. I simply know that you can't be resilient if you are not healthy, and you can't be healthy without good nutrition. Figure out what works for you.

Luckily, there are loads of people and resources available to help you do this.

Eat well!

Everything in Moderation

In researching this topic, I found someone who makes a great deal of sense to me, but seems to miss the mark at the same time. She sounds just like my grandmothers, who said things like, "everything in moderation." They knew how to eat properly, and so does Marion Nestle, professor in the Department of Nutrition, Food Studies, and Public Health at New York University.[47]

Marion gives the following advice regarding eating well:

- eat fruits and vegetables

- avoid junk food

- balance your caloric intake with your level of activity

- avoid processed foods to the extent that you can

According to Marion, "It really isn't any more complicated than that."

I agree. Sort of.

For many of us, it is more complicated. Eating well is not just about common-sense thinking. We know that we find ourselves searching through the kitchen or stopping by the store to find foods we should *not* eat. We also find ourselves deciding before a meal that we are *not* going to eat dessert, only to end up eating an enormous piece of cake after a filling meal.

> Let's face it, eating well is sometimes more about our emotional health than our knowledge of nutrition.

Of course, Marion is right. And for some people, this strategy works.

If I put cookies on the counter for George to take in his lunch, he sets them aside and says, "Thanks, but I don't need these." To which I say, "You need to take them out of the house, because I'm working at home and I will eat them all."

281

I recall a day following a birthday celebration the night before. It was *my* birthday, after all, and I was left at home alone with half a chocolate cake. It was a 10-inch round cake; so, let's assume there were about six cups of cake left.

You know where I'm going with this…

David came home at the end of the day and asked where the cake was. I told him, in all honesty, "I ate it." He said, "You did not eat that whole cake?" I assured him that I did. By the way, I did not sit down with a fork and eat the cake out of the box. I cut small pieces, put them on plates, and ate them with a fork, in a very civilized manner. I started at nine-thirty in the morning. By the time I ate the sixth piece, it was late afternoon.

It's Not Just About Awareness

I'm well aware of the fundamentals of nutrition. I know how we are supposed to eat. I just don't have much willpower when it comes to food; especially the foods I consider "comfort foods". I don't think I'm alone.

This is where, from a resilience perspective, physical health links back to emotional health. I can't be physically healthy unless I am in control of my emotions. For those who struggle in this way, we need to find a strategy that works for us. For me, the best strategy has been to create a "positive circle". This is the opposite of a "vicious circle", where I begin to fall away from my good habits and all hell breaks loose from a health perspective. I need to do several good things that support my physical health, and these elements work together to keep me on track.

Here's how it works for me:

- **I exercise.** I keep a regular schedule of getting my body moving. This might be 3 to 4 times a week. It is not too long, nor too onerous – or I won't do it. I try to find things I enjoy doing, like cycling, but I'll settle for things I don't hate, like the treadmill with a good show to watch.

- **I go to my favorite "weigh-in" spot.** That's the place you pay to go and step on a scale in front of another person, usually a nice lady who knows what you are going through, because she has been there herself. Now, I don't want to promote any particular business, but the one that has worked for me requires that I step on a scale and record my weight. If I'm where I should be in my weight, I only go once a month, and it's free. If I have weight to lose, I go every week, and it costs money. This process holds me accountable to that scale. It also puts me in the same room as some people who can help inspire me to lose my weight, and give me tools to do it.

- **As part of this program, I also write down everything I eat.** This makes me aware of what I'm eating and how many calories are involved. I can eat whatever I want, but I have to write it down. There is a recommended level of caloric intake for me and I try to stay at or near this level.

- **I dress in clothes that fit.** Now this might sound nuts, but for me, wearing clothes that accentuate my curves makes me more aware of the gift that my body provides. It is there for me and allows me to do the things I want to do in this world. If it is a little bigger, or a little smaller, that's okay. I have clothes that fit my body in different states.

The critical point for me is that I don't hide my body under big, ill-fitting clothing so no one, including me, can see it. I don't wear men's t-shirts. They are made for men. I don't wear tights and a long top, because I can put on twenty pounds under there before anyone notices.

I need a reality check and I need to own that, although my body is wonderful at any size, if I'm gaining weight, I want to make a change of some kind. I wear clothes that fit and look good on my body. That makes me feel good and keeps me on track. I would recommend that men avoid the huge t-shirt and track pants method of dressing, as this will create the same sneaky weight gain problem.

When I put these four things together, I end up with a winning recipe for success. I'm not perfect, but I try to stick to these ideas. When I "fall off the wagon" – and I do – I can just focus on any one of them and the rest tend to follow. I'm not keen to go to weigh in until I work out a few times and feel better about myself. The scale is not going to be significantly different after three days of working out, but I will feel okay with the number on the scale because I know I'm on the right track. I actually want to weigh in then, so that I can see where I'm starting.

If you are my husband George or Marion Nestle, you can just use logic and good nutritional information to manage your eating. If you are more like me, you will need to find strategies that work for you. Once you find something that works, stick to it. If you need help finding a winning strategy, look to www.theresilienceway.com for some resources.

The Future of Food

Some of the most exciting developments in the world of nutrition are not new at all. You may be noticing the media is now full of information about "food as medicine". It is interesting that we are now clearly linking diet to healing. We are recognizing the links between what we eat and the diseases we get. This is not a new idea.

> Most of the ideas being proposed now have existed in traditional Chinese and Indian medicine, and in the healing knowledge of indigenous peoples the world over.

As we move forward, I believe we will see in Western culture a better understanding and acceptance of foods that can help with each disease or illness. I believe we will also begin to link food and nutrition to genetic information in order to create food recommendations that are completely personalized. With this knowledge, we can use the basics of nutrition to ensure we are as healthy as possible, and to avoid or treat illness.

As I looked back at what David was eating prior to being diagnosed with colon cancer, I wondered about some of his food choices. I wonder, in particular, about the nitrates contained in many of the foods he ate. I really try to curb the number of nitrates we consume. As soon as David was diagnosed, I started searching for information about how foods might help or hinder his recovery. I found a book that recommended a list of "anti-cancer foods".[48]

You can easily find this list, but generally, it recommends:

- vegetables from the cabbage family (cabbage, brussels sprouts, broccoli and cauliflower)

- orange vegetables (carrots, sweet potatoes, squash)

- citrus fruits (oranges, lemons and grapefruits)

- berries (strawberries, raspberries, blueberries, blackberries, cranberries)

- certain spices (including turmeric and cinnamon)

I recall thinking, many times over the course of our cancer treatment journey, that with all efforts to cure David with chemotherapy, there was never any advice or direction as to what foods he should eat or not eat. I just don't think it was part of the treatment plan, and so it never came up. In the future, I imagine that this will not be the case. I expect that we will learn more, and our medical professionals will be more comfortable making recommendations about our food choices. Food will become part of the healing process.

Exercise

How Exercise Builds Resilience

In normal times, exercise is critical to becoming and remaining healthy and active.

> When times get tough, the stress-relieving effects of exercise are an important way to build resilience.

If the issue we face is a health issue, we want to enter that situation with the highest fitness level possible.

We need to:

- Keep active in our day to day lives by looking for simple ways to increase our exercise and activity levels.

- Find safe and enjoyable ways to build cardiovascular health and flexibility, so we maintain our ability to remain active as we age.

- Consider factors that encourage us to be less active, including screen time and sitting at work. What can we do to get moving instead?

- Find professional help from a doctor and/or fitness professional, when in doubt, in order to find safe and effective ways to improve your fitness levels.

According to a report prepared by the Mental Health Foundation in the United Kingdom,[49] physical exercise has an impact on:

- Positive moods. Studies have found that even just a 10-15-minute walk had a positive impact on mood states.

- Stress. People are reporting higher and higher levels of stress in their daily lives. This stress causes the "fight or flight" chemicals, adrenaline and noradrenaline, to raise blood pressure and increase heart rates. It can also reduce the efficiency of the immune system. Studies have shown a positive impact on stress management from physical exercise.

- Self-esteem. People who exercise regularly report increased levels of self-esteem.

- Depression & Anxiety. Physical exercise has consistently shown to be effective in the reduction of symptoms of both of these conditions.

- Sleep. People who are physically active report better sleep quality. People who had previous sleep difficulties, reported reductions in insomnia and pre-sleep anxiety as a result of fifty minutes of exercise, three times a week.

Exercise for Your Brain

Dr. Wendy Suzuki, a Professor of Neural Science and Psychology in the Center for Neural Science at New York University, is also an author, storyteller and fitness instructor. Several years ago, she began an experiment on herself. She was finding that despite her successful career as a neuroscientist she was not happy. She had no social life and did not have a healthy lifestyle. When she went on a rafting trip, she discovered she was the weakest person on the boat.

This was a turning point for her. She decided to make exercise part of her life.

The result was a complete change to her life, both personally and professionally. She ended up changing her entire research focus to look at the effects of regular exercise on our brains.

The first thing she found was a growing body of literature that was essentially showing everything that she had noticed in herself. People who exercise regularly experience better mood, better energy, better memory, and better attention.

Exercise has three impacts on our brains:

1. First, it has an immediate, but short-lived effect on your brain. A single workout will **increase your mood** immediately. Dr. Suzuki's research showed that "a single workout can improve your ability to shift and focus attention, and that focus improvement will last for at least two hours." You can also expect **improved reaction times**.

2. Second, an exercise regime that increases your cardio-respiratory function will give

you longer-lasting effects, including the **production of new brain cells** that actually increase the brain's volume, which **improves long-term memory, focus and attentiveness**. These improvements are less transient and have long-term benefits.

3. Perhaps the most important thing that exercise does is **protect your brain**. If you think about the brain like a muscle, it follows that the more you exercise, the bigger and stronger your brain becomes. This is important, because when the brain grows, it expands the prefrontal cortex and the hippocampus, the two areas most susceptible to neurodegenerative diseases and normal cognitive decline in aging. According to Dr. Suzuki, "...with increased exercise over your lifetime, you're not going to cure dementia or Alzheimer's disease, but...you're going to **create the strongest, biggest hippocampus and prefrontal cortex** so it takes longer for these diseases to actually have an effect."

> "You can think of exercise as a supercharged (savings plan) for your brain."

So clearly, our resilience is affected by exercise.

We need to keep up our cardiovascular fitness in order to do the things we want to do. We need an exercise regime to deliver the short and long-term benefits of better moods, memory, focus and attention, and to protect our brains from disease as we age.

Some People Love Exercise

Often, I have been tempted to remove this entire element from The Resilience Way. But not because I don't think it's important. It's just because I'm bad at it. I'm good at sleeping, but nutrition and exercise are my "areas for improvement".

When it comes to exercise, I have been generally active throughout my life. In fact, at some points, I was very active and fit. As a child, I was an athlete; as a young woman, I was a fitness instructor. I taught fitness classes right up until I delivered my second baby.

So, what happened?

I became less and less active as I became more and more busy with life. Just like so many folks, right? Now, I struggle to stay on track with my exercise and workout often enough. Once I get going, I'm not too bad, but when I stop the routine of regular exercise, it can be hard to get started again.

I'm in awe of people who can stick to regular exercise and seem to actually enjoy it. I was curious about what made these people "tick" and so I searched for some insights.

Here is what I found out about people who love to exercise.[50]

1. They only exercise in ways they enjoy

People who love to exercise don't waste time with activities they despise. They find an activity, class or program they like and they stick to it. They understand that if they try to force themselves to do something they don't like; they will

291

find any excuse to skip their workouts. If you are anything like me, you are good at finding those excuses.

2. They use a device to track their progress

Those who exercise regularly like the instant feedback that their fitness trackers provide. You may already have a device. Or maybe you have noticed people with tracking devices on their wrists or phones. Whether tracking your heartrate, calories, time spent, or distance travelled, these devices can help motivate you to push yourself further or exceed your personal best.

For many of my friends, the love/hate relationship they have with their fitness tracker does get them off the couch and reaching their fitness goals each day.

3. They exercise with a friend

For most people, it is more fun to exercise with a friend. You are much less apt to ditch your workout if your friend is expecting you to go with them. A running buddy can keep your pace going, even if you would rather slow down.

In my case, I know that if I don't get out of bed and hit the treadmill, then George does not exercise either. I feel guilty, so I get up. Oh, the wonders of guilt! For those without a workout buddy in their bed, you could also find one by joining a local running or biking club or signing up for a recreational sports league.

4. They go outside

There are studies that show that half an hour a day out in nature is good for both our physical and mental health. For me, this is just common sense. I live in the country and I notice the opposite when I'm in the city. After a day in a city, I'm clamoring to get back to the farm for some fresh air and green living things.

In one 2011 study, sweating outdoors was associated with a boost of energy, more engagement in the activity, and better mental well-being[51]. In the spring, summer and fall, I turn in my treadmill for my road bike, and all of a sudden, I'm not exercising, I'm just having fun.

5. They don't fuss about missing a workout

Everyone misses workouts. That's life. Things come up. If you beat yourself up about a missed workout, you are actually less likely to stay on track overall. After all, who wants to do something that might mean being scolded? That negative feeling can tend to affect your future exercise plans.

It's like when I "fall off the wagon" in exercise terms. I get so upset with myself that I don't even want to think about exercise. However, if I set a reasonable goal, say a certain number of workouts per week, I'm much more likely to stick to it.

Personally, I have also found that I'm much less likely to do a workout if it is too intense, as in every moment past 30 minutes that I'm still on the treadmill.

6. They don't focus on weight loss

Focusing on weight loss will tend to bring a negative mindset to your workouts and make it harder for you to stay on track. However, if you keep your focus on longer-term, more powerful goals, like living to see your kids get married or preparing for an adventure vacation, you will be more motivated to stay active.

7. They find creative ways to exercise

I actually don't like my treadmill. But I like it more than most of the other options that are readily available to me. In the summertime I love to bike ride and a Sunday morning ride of about fifty kilometers is a joy. I love to take a new route and see some new sights.

Those who are better at sticking to their exercise regimes find interesting ways to exercise. The goal is to raise your heartrate and keep it raised for a while. How you do that is up to you. You may find that joining a sports team works or you may find that taking the stairs instead of the elevator adds a new challenge. No rules.

8. They set goals and reward themselves

We have talked about goal setting before, and our exercise goals should link to our overall goals.

If you have set a goal for improving your fitness level, that goal will help keep you going by informing you as to why you should get out of bed or off the couch, and do that workout.

When you do follow through on your exercise plans, you should reward yourself in some way to mark your progress toward the goal. A small, but specific to the goal, treat will encourage you to follow through with your exercise intentions, and reach your goals.

The next two stories demonstrate how physical exercise built resilience into the lives of two people. Their life stories are different, their approach to fitness is different, but they both benefit from incorporating exercise into their lives. It has allowed them to move through some tough times.[52]

A Former Marine's Story

A soldier in the Marine Corps Infantry, Mike Ergo, served two tours in Iraq, much of which he spent fighting on the front lines. When he returned to the U.S. in 2005, having lost so many close friends, he had no idea where to go next. "I didn't expect to come home alive," he says, "so trying to plan a whole new life was difficult."

Ergo ended up turning to drugs and alcohol to deal with his PTSD. "I think I was just living for that next good feeling, which for me, usually came in a bottle," says Ergo, who married his wife, Sara, shortly after returning from Iraq. It wasn't until July 2012 that Sara sat Ergo down and told him he wasn't the man she married. She challenged him to make a change. "I had a moment of clarity...and just quit cold turkey," Ergo says.

In search of something to turn his attention to, Ergo started doing CrossFit. Then, a friend asked him to join a half-marathon, so he laced up and started running. He immediately fell for his experience on the road.

> "I remember thinking: 'I'm putting my body through stress, and my body's handling it. I have all these internal resources to deal with this — I don't need external chemicals to regulate my mood.'"

Not too long after this, a friend invited Ergo to an Alcatraz swim in the San Francisco Bay. Within that same year, while on vacation in Hawaii, Ergo watched the Ironman World Championships. This is an extreme contest where competitors complete a two-mile swim, 112-mile bike ride, and a marathon-distance run. He signed up for a half-Ironman as soon as he got home.

"I have a history in the Marine Corps of putting myself through discomfort and finding satisfaction and purpose in that, as opposed to just looking for easy and comfortable," he says. He figured a triathlon would be no different, and completed that first race in 2015. He then did a few more half-Ironman triathlons in 2016. In the fall of 2017, he committed to a full Ironman back in Hawaii.

Thanks to the tough training sessions and grueling Ironman courses, Ergo has also learned to be okay with things not being 100 percent all the time and has taken a softer approach to dealing with hardships.

"At first, I think I approached it with a sense of 'I'm going to beat this, I'm going to overcome it' — a really aggressive attitude. It's more like what I'd say as a CrossFitter," he says. "But it's hard to crush something for 13 hours. [My new approach] was really just gratitude, and acceptance of where I am. To think about being on the finish line, and being done after 12 or 13 hours, that's mentally taxing. That means for 12 or 13 hours, you're not where you want to be… So, I'm always coming back to: 'This is okay. I can hurt. That's fine."

"It's about making peace with discomfort, and that translates into everyday life — not needing things to be ideal all the time, because they aren't."

He continues, "If you can have the discipline in whatever the workout routine is, and put yourself through some adversity and some discomfort, then when that comes up in other avenues in life, you're ready for it."

Krista's Story

Krista Meinert had never exercised regularly; although, in her adult life she started adding daily yoga sessions to her schedule. She loved the mind-body connection and how it seemed to slow things down, while also strengthening her core.

But that all changed on January 10, 2010.

While her son Jake was serving in Afghanistan, he stepped on an explosive device and died. "Nothing is the same after that. Jake's death changed many aspects of my life,"

Meinert says. "My firstborn was gone. I didn't know who I was anymore. At the same time, I didn't want to be labeled as the mother of a dead son."

Fast-forward a few years, when Meinert found herself looking through old photos. "I noticed in the pictures I was in since Jake's death that I had been smiling in them, but it was an empty smile — there was no feeling behind it," says the 47-year-old.

She did spot one photo from 2013, though, with her daughter and niece, standing on the top of Mt. Cloundry in Colorado. "That was the first real smile I had after [my son] died."

Not long after finding that photo, Meinert received an email from TAPS — an organization that offers support to people who lost a loved one in the military. They were hosting an expedition with REI Adventures to Mt. Shasta in California. Meinert knew she had to go.

She started researching training plans to prepare for her trek. Upper and lower body workouts soon became a regular to-do, and she began carrying a 40- to 60-pound backpack wherever she could. "It got me out of my comfort zone and thinking about other things besides how miserable I was," Meinert says.

In 2016, she reached the top of Mt. Shasta.

Besides the beauty of seeing the stars at night and the sunrise as she reached the summit, Meinert made life-long friends during that climb and found something that brought her real joy. "I love the planning of it and I love the experience of working with a team, and the focus on survival," she says. And because she was with a group of other TAPS members, she had great listeners to share her story. "I think we all felt really comfortable talking about our broken hearts," she says.

Since the Mt. Shasta climb, Meinert has summited 19 of the 50 U.S. state high points. And she has no plans of stopping. "The effects of exercising and mountaineering is that I actually have a life now. After I lost my son, I felt like I wasn't living," Meinert says. "Exercise and mountaineering let me be in the moment. If I miss my step, I'm going to slide. So, I have to make sure I'm present, not in the past being sad. I'm not in the future, wishing things were different. I'm right there and I'm excited and I'm nervous."

Meinert says this has translated into her being a better mother to her other children, too. "Even mothering my other kids, I was in a haze, a grieving haze," she says.

> "The climbing got me out of that haze. It got me out of that dark place and it made me be back to who I was. It's also gotten me excited about a future."

Two things she has to look forward to? Summiting Mt. Hood in Oregon and Half Dome in Yosemite National Park this summer.

These two stories demonstrate the power of physical exercise in creating resilience. They show two people who overcame enormous challenges, partly because they learned to move their bodies. They found focus, purpose, and accomplishment in exercise. It kept them grounded and showed them the path forward.

They are great examples of resilience.

PHYSICAL HEALTH

Sleep · Nutrition · Exercise

In this chapter we talked about:

Sleep

A Good Night's Sleep – don't underestimate the value of sleep

Don't Fall into Bad Habits – are you doing things that you will regret later?

A Chance to Dream – pay attention to those first moments when you wake

Nutrition

Everything in Moderation – just like my grandmothers advised

It's Not Just About Awareness – you may have some habits to explore

The Future of Food – continue to learn about foods that are going to help you stay healthy

Exercise

Exercise for your Brain – it's not just your body that benefits. There are huge gains for your brain

Some People Love Exercise – what can we learn from them?

For more information please visit:
www.theresilienceway.com

Chapter Ten

Next Steps

What's Next?

Now what? What do we do with all these stories? How can we make sense of The Resilience Way in our own lives? What should we do next?

It seems to me that learning about what is possible is the easy part. Learning about resilience and seeing examples of how others have built and used resilience is not hard. Putting this learning to use in your own life is the hard part. Figuring out what you need to change, and then making the change is hard. Sticking to the new ways is even harder. We talked about this in the section about **Learning Focus**. Now, it's time to make it happen.

But first, there's time for one more quote:

> "Grant me the serenity to accept the things I cannot change, the courage to change the things I can, and the wisdom to know the difference."

This is the ever-fabulous and slightly adapted *Serenity Prayer,* generally attributed to the Protestant theologian, Reinhold Niebuhr. I learned it in grade-school and try to remember it when I find myself trying to change something I can't. This poem helps me focus on the present, on the things I *can* control, on making necessary changes in my life. It stops me from finding excuses and wallowing in self-pity. It stops me from blaming others or "bad luck" for the things I don't like in my life. It encourages me to find solutions. It is just such a gem.

With that in mind, the best way to move forward in the context of this book is to follow the steps below.

Step One: Reflection

In Chapter Four, there is a short evaluation of your resilience elements. If you have not already completed this assessment, it's time to do so. If you have, review what you learned, and consider any changes you would make, based on the learning you have done since Chapter Four. This will give you the chance to see where you have strengths and where you need to focus your efforts to build resilience. Be as honest with yourself as possible in this evaluation, so you can get usable data for the next step.

Now… focus first on what you do well. Write down the elements you consider strengths, then jot down your thoughts about why you think these are strengths. What makes you good at this particular element? What are some examples of you using this element as a strength? How has this served you well?

Here's an example:

David would have considered **Values Clarity** to be a strength…

- **Examples of this element as a strength:**

  His behavior never deviated from his strong values of supporting people, finding meaningful work, and creating a stable, loving environment for his wife and children.

- **Outcome of this element as a strength:**

  He did not have to wonder what to do in most situations. His values drove his behavior. He felt grounded in this set of values and they increased his resilience.

Now, focus on the elements that you want to improve. Write them down, and then write about how weakness in this area is impacting your life. What are some examples of how this is getting in your way?

Here's an example:

I consider **Self-Awareness** to be an area to improve...

- **Some examples of this element needing improvement:**

  Sometimes I let other people "push my buttons" and I get wound up in worrying about situations where I feel others are not being fair or kind.

- **This has impact in my life in the following ways:**

  I build up grudges and carry around upset that drains my energy and interferes with my resilience. I can't focus on the things I really want to do in order to live my dreams, because I'm spending my time and energy on past transgressions.

This process of reflection will help you see where your resilience is grounded. It will help you to understand that you already have developed resilience in some areas. It will also help you recognize where you want to improve, and why.

> The why is important because identifying how something is interfering with your resilience will give you the energy to make the necessary changes.

Step Two: Action Planning

Now that you have thought through your resilience with respect to your strengths and areas for improvement, you are ready to think about creating an action plan.

Think about using your strengths to help you tackle changes you want to make. I, for instance, am good at seeking support from others and not so great at keeping to my exercise regime. I ask for help from friends and family in helping me stay on track. The buddy system is my key tool for keeping to my exercise schedule. I never want to workout, but I *will* do it if it sounds more like a social engagement than an opportunity to sweat. So, as I plan around increasing or sticking to my workouts, I create action plans that involve others.

Review all of the areas where you want to improve, then list the changes you want to make. Choose two or three of these changes to focus on first. You can't change everything all at once.

Figure out which are your starting points. It might be that these two or three things are the ones that are most important or are getting in the way most. Or, it may be that they are easy hitters – things you can accomplish quickly and easily that will give you the energy to tackle the tougher stuff.

Try using a format like this:

Element/Area of Focus	Which of the five Elements do you want to improve? Or, which Factors do you want to improve within an Element?
Specific Action Steps	What are the specific, measurable steps you will take to improve?
Planned Completion Date	When will each step be completed?
Quick Hits to Get Started	What can you do within the next couple of weeks or months (for longer steps) that will get you started?

You may have heard before about the concept of SMART objectives. Well, that's what we are looking for when we write down our action steps.

They need to be **S**pecific, **M**easurable, **A**ttainable, **R**elevant and **T**imed.

It helps me if I think about having to prove to someone else that the task is completed as planned. Imagine that you are doing a performance review at work. Can you prove that the actions you agreed to take are really complete? Some tasks are easy to measure. If you plan to complete the Personal Values Exercise, and then you do it and have the notes to prove it —clearly, it's done.

However, if you plan to place boundaries around a relationship that is getting in the way of your resilience, then you will need to think about how that could be measured. It's harder to measure, but not impossible.

For instance, I would need to plan a few steps as a framework for my boundary building. I might plan to journal about options for designing a better relationship with the person, plan to have a conversation with the person, and set a date for these steps and the final decision about the new arrangement to be implemented.

So, there are three action steps here. In the end, the outside world might see only the conversation that happened, while the rest is just my work. But I know the work got done, because I set up the measurement when I planned the action steps. In this way, I can't just keep avoiding the situation.

Before getting into planning your action steps, you will also want to review the section in Chapter Eight around **Learning Focus**.

If you remember, in this section we talked about how to change habits and how to dig deep into what is going to get in your way. If you want to change a habit, you need to understand what is driving you to love the habit you have, so you can drop it and allow a different habit to become your norm.

You also need to explore the fears and assumptions that can keep you from being able to make a change stick.

Step Three: Implement with Celebration

If you do a great job on the first two steps, then the rest is easier. If you get to Step Three with a clear understanding of the steps you want to take, and some thoughts about what might get in your way, then you are ready to roll.

Once you get to implementing, it is really just about keeping your action plans close and reviewing them often to ensure you are on track. You should only have two or three items you are working on; so perhaps ten action items in total. You can manage these easily.

Celebration is also a critical way to stay on track. Remember to celebrate your accomplishments along the way. Tell others about your achievements. Journal about the changes you have made. These actions are a big deal and you need to celebrate them. Rewards and celebrations give you the energy to keep improving while maintaining the improvements you have made.

Step Four: Review & Adjust

As you implement your plans, you are ready to add more and new action plans. Go back to your notes from Step One and find your next areas for development. Consider how the implementation of your first set of plans went. What worked well? What got in your way?

Now, create new action plans in the same way as before. Make sure they are specific and measurable. Plan how you will celebrate or reward yourself for their completion, or the steps along the way.

And Finally...

Be kind to yourself.

As you attempt to make changes, you will falter. This is not all easy. You will find some things that can be changed fairly quickly and easily, but you will also find areas that are really tough.

If you decide to tackle some of those tough areas, make sure you plan carefully and think about who can support you. And also, how you can break it down into smaller pieces.

309

Some of the things in the way of you building resilience are grounded in habits formed a long time ago; these will take considerable time and effort to change.

But... they *can* be changed. You just have to figure out how.

The resources on **The Resilience Way** website (www.theresilienceway.com) will help. Loads of other online resources are also available. Find what you need, work on a few things at a time, and you will see progress. You will be living your life with an authenticity and tenacity that allows resilience to grow.

Chapter Eleven

Moving Forward

Keep In Touch

It is my absolute pleasure to be able to share **The Resilience Way** with you. I am so blessed to have had a rich life and many experiences that taught me how to be strong, to grow from my experience, and to follow my dreams. I am blessed to have known a wonderful man who lived his short life as a role model for resilience.

This book has introduced you to **The Resilience Way**, a model and method for developing the resilience you need in life. I hope that it resonates with you and helps you to see your areas of strength and areas needing improvement. We all have both.

The Resilience Way is a personal journey for each of us and everyone's journey to resilience will be different. Fortunately, resilience is learnable and contains a specific set of Elements and Factors that can be created and developed. You just have to commit.

Along the way, you will need help. You can find that in the conversations and resources available through www.theresilienceway.com

Please join us to share your story and learn from others. Brew a cup of coffee or tea and meet us there.

Acknowledgements

First and foremost, I want to thank my family for all their support throughout my journey.

My Mom, Myrna, has been an unbelievable support throughout my life, no matter what challenge we faced. She is selfless to a fault and just the best!

My fantastic children keep me grounded by always pointing out where I'm messing up and offering corrections. They amaze me and inspire me every day. They each carry David's spirit in their own way, and I just love it.

George has been an enormous help as a sounding board, thinking partner, and critique. He has patiently offered love, support and good advice.

There are many more family members who deserve a mention. You know who you are. Thanks!

So many of my dear friends deserve a mention, too. Yvette and Jeff have been my rocks from the start. Terri has been my no-nonsense reality check and creative director. Mel has reminded me that mine is a story worth sharing, and that others will benefit from hearing it. Donna invited me to join book club; and in doing so, added so many wonderful people to my life. Kimberley served George to me on a silver platter and has always been there to offer her help.

And there are so many more…

Going back a bit further, I want to thank David's medical team, including Sandra Ferris, RN, Georgina McCulloch, RN, Dr. Catherine (Kate) Anderson, Dr. Tina Williams and Dr. Greg Knight. You all made an impossible situation as hopeful as it could be and offered the best of yourselves in the process.

I'm grateful to the universe for bringing me my Editor, Maria D'Marco, my research psychologist, Emma Conway, and my graphic designer, Terri Dennis Hobson.

the RESILIENCE WAY

EMOTIONAL WELL-BEING

Self-Awareness · Mental Wellness · Spirituality

SUPPORTIVE RELATIONSHIPS

Seek Support · Support Others · Boundaries

PERSONAL CLARITY

Personal Values · Personal Vision · Planning

DYNAMIC THINKING

Confidence · Realism · Learning Focus

PHYSICAL HEALTH

Sleep · Nutrition · Exercise

Index

319

Endnotes

1. J.M. Twenge et al., "Birth cohort increases in psychopathology among young Americans, 1938–2007: A cross-temporal meta-analysis of the MMPI," *Clinical Psychology Review* 30 (2010): 145–154, http://www-personal.umich.edu/~daneis/symposium/2010/ARTICLES/twenge_2010.pdf

2. Bronnie Ware, *The Top Five Regrets of the Dying*, (Hay House Inc., 2012)

3. Wayne Dyer, *The Essential Wayne Dyer Collection*, (Hay House Inc., 2013), Kindle edition: 192-193.

4. Lion's Roar Staff, "Buddhist Teachings on Mindfulness Meditation," *Lion's Roar*, (Lion's Roar Foundation), https://www.lionsroar.com/buddhist-teachings-on-mindfulness-meditation/

5. John Lennon, From the song *Beautiful Boy (Darling Boy)*

6. Matthieu Ricard, "The Habits of Happiness," filmed February 2004 in Monterey, CA, USA, TED video, 20:51, https://www.ted.com/talks/matthieu_ricard_on_the_habits_of_happiness#t-10290.

7. Dan Gilbert, "The Surprising Science of Happiness," filmed February 2004 in Monterey, CA, USA, TED video, 21:01, https://www.ted.com/talks/dan_gilbert_asks_why_are_we_happy.

8. Robert Emmons, "Why Gratitude Is Good," *Greater Good Magazine*, Berkeley, University of California, https://greatergood.berkeley.edu/article/item/why_gratitude_is_good

9. "What is Gratitude," *Psychology Today*, https://www.psychologytoday.com/ca/basics/gratitude

10. Romeo Dallaire, *Waiting for First Light: My Ongoing Battle with PTSD,* (Toronto: Random House Canada, a division of Penguin Random House Canada Limited, 2016), Kindle edition: 45-46.

11. Thomas Attig, How We Grieve, New York: Oxford University Press, Inc., 2011.

12. World Health Organization, "Mental health: a state of well-being," World Health Organization, (2014), https://www.who.int/features/factfiles/mentalhealth/en/

13. Bernard Corfe and Lauren Owen, "The role of diet and nutrition on mental health and wellbeing," Proceedings of the Nutrition Society, Volume 76, Issue 4, (2017): 425, https://www.cambridge.org/core/journals/proceedings-of-the-nutrition-society/article/role-of-diet-and-nutrition-on-mental-health-and-wellbeing/372284768DB78DB02EB199E277AABF79

14. Dr. Sarah Edmunds, Hannah Biggs and Isabella Goldie, "Let's get physical," Mental Health Foundation, United

Kingdom, (2013),
https://www.mentalhealth.org.uk/sites/default/files/le
ts-get-physical-report.pdf

15. Mayo Clinic, Postpartum Depression, Symptoms &
    causes. https://www.mayoclinic.org/diseases-
    conditions/postpartum-depression/symptoms-
    causes/syc-20376617

16. Dallaire, Waiting for First Light, 78

17. Ibid., 40-41.

18. Ibid., 46.

19. Ibid., 73.

20. Ibid., 174-175.

21. A. Tom Horvath, Ph.D., Abpp, Kaushik Misra, Ph.D.,
    Amy K. Epner, Ph.D., Galen Morgan Cooper, Ph.D.,
    "Definition of Addiction", MentalHelp.net,
    https://www.mentalhelp.net/articles/definition-of-
    addiction/

22. BBC iWonder, "Are we wired to believe in a higher
    power?", The BBC,
    http://www.bbc.co.uk/guides/z3b6hyc

23. Yonat Shimron, "Most Americans believe in a higher
    power, but not always in the God of the bible", The
    Washington Post, (2018),
    https://www.washingtonpost.com/news/acts-of-
    faith/wp/2018/04/25/most-americans-believe-in-a-

higher-power-but-not-always-in-the-god-of-the-bible/?noredirect=on&utm_term=.d530aac132a3

24. Graeme Hamilton, "Canadians may be vacating the pews but they are keeping the faith: poll," National Post, (2017), https://nationalpost.com/news/canada/canadians-may-be-vacating-the-pews-but-they-are-keeping-the-faith-poll

25. Ben Clements, *Surveying Christian Beliefs and Religious Debates in Post-War Britain*, (Hampshire: Palgrave MacMillan, 2016).

26. "As Cameron says UK "still a Christian country", 62% tell YouGov they are "not religious," National Secular Society, (2015), https://www.secularism.org.uk/news/2015/04/as-cameron-says-uk-still-a-christian-country-62-percent-tell-yougov-they-are-not-religious

27. Cindy Miller-Perrin, Elizabeth Krumrei Mancuso, *Faith from a Positive Psychology Perspective*, (Springer, 2015).

28. David Masci and Michael Lipka, "Americans may be getting less religious, but feelings of spirituality are on the rise," Pew Research Centre, (2015), https://www.pewresearch.org/fact-tank/2016/01/21/americans-spirituality/

29. His Holiness The Dalai Lama, *In My Own Words – An introduction to my teachings and philosophy*, (Hay House, Inc., 2008), 151.

30. BJ Miller, "We fear death, but what if dying isn't as bad as we think?", The Guardian, (2017), https://www.theguardian.com/science/blog/2017/jul/25/we-fear-death-but-what-if-dying-isnt-as-bad-as-we-think

31. Shoba Sreenivasan, Ph.D., Linda E. Weinberger, Ph.D., "Emotional Nourishment - Why We Need Each Other," *Psychology Today*, (2016), https://www.psychologytoday.com/ca/blog/emotional-nourishment/201612/why-we-need-each-other

32. His Holiness The Dalai Lama, *In My Own Words*, 2

33. Women of Courage. Rogers TV, Woodstock, Ontario. Hosted by Anne Miner. https://youtu.be/Jm-ID1XbD-s?t=9s

34. Michelle Obama, "Remarks by the First Lady at Tuskegee University Commencement Address," Tuskegee University, Tuskegee, Alabama, May 09, 2015, https://obamawhitehouse.archives.gov/the-press-office/2015/05/09/remarks-first-lady-tuskegee-university-commencement-address

35. Viktor Frankl, *Man's Search for Meaning*, (Boston: Beacon Press, 2006), Kindle Edition: 105.

36. Lewis Carroll, *Alice's Adventures in Wonderland*, Kindle edition, Chapter 6.

37. Extract from I am Prepared to Die – Mandela's statement from the dock at the opening of the defence case in the Rivonia Trial, Pretoria Supreme Court, 20

April 1964, https://www.sbs.com.au/news/transcript-nelson-mandela-speech-i-am-prepared-to-die

38. Nelson Mandela, *Long Walk to Freedom: The Autobiography of Nelson Mandela*, (Philadelphia: Little Brown & Co., 1994), 750.

39. Frankl, *Man's Search for Meaning,* 103-104.

40. Sheryl Sandberg & Adam Grant, *Option B – Facing Adversity, Building Resilience and Finding Joy*, (New York: Alfred A. Knopf, a division of Penguin Random House LLC, 2017), 91.

41. C.R. Snyder, "Hope Theory: Rainbows in the mind", *Psychological Inquiry*, 2002, Vol. 13, No. 4, 249, https://www.tandfonline.com/doi/abs/10.1207/S15327965PLI1304_01

42. Snyder, C. R., Harris, C., Anderson, J. R., Holleran, S. A., Irving, L. M., Sigmon, S. T., Yoshinobu, L. R., Gibb, J., Langelle, C., & Harney, P., "The will and the ways: Development of an individual-differences measure of hope," *Journal of Personality and Social Psychology*, (1991), 60, 570–585.

43. Teri Goetz, "How to Change Unhealthy Habits," *Psychology Today*, (2016), https://www.psychologytoday.com/ca/blog/renaissance-woman/201607/how-change-unhealthy-habits

44. Robert Kegan & Lisa Laskow Lahey, *Immunity to Change: How to overcome it and unlock the potential in yourself and your*

organization, (Boston: Harvard Business Review Press, 2009).

45. Jean-Louis et al., "Sleep and quality of well-being," SLEEP, Vol. 23, No. 8, (2000), https://www.ncbi.nlm.nih.gov/pubmed/11145326

46. "Sleep Matters – The impact of sleep on health and wellbeing," Mental Health Foundation, United Kingdom, https://www.mentalhealth.org.uk/publications/sleep-report

47. Jon Stewart, "A conversation with Marion Nestle: Straight talk about obesity, nutrition and food policy," *The Permanante Journal*, (2006), https://www.ncbi.nlm.nih.gov/pmc/articles/PMC3078787/

48. David Servan-Schreiber, *Anticancer, A New Way of Life*, (Paris: Harper Collins Publishers Ltd, 2007), 133.

49. Dr. Sarah Edmunds, Hannah Biggs and Isabella Goldie, "Let's get physical," Mental Health Foundation, United Kingdom, (2013), https://www.mentalhealth.org.uk/sites/default/files/lets-get-physical-report.pdf

50. Jessica Migala, "10 Habits of People Who Love to Work Out," Health.com, (2015), https://www.health.com/health/gallery/0,,20907868,00.html

51. J. Thompson Coon, K. Boddy, K. Stein, R. Whear, J. Barton, M. H. Depledge. "Does Participating in

Physical Activity in Outdoor Natural Environments Have a Greater Effect on Physical and Mental Wellbeing than Physical Activity Indoors? A Systematic Review", *Environmental Science & Technology*, 2011.

52. Mallory Creveling, "How Exercise Changed These 7 People's Lives," *Daily Burn*, (2018), https://www.google.com/search?q=how+exercise+changed+these+7+people%27s+lives&rlz=1C1CHBF_enCA705CA705&oq=how+exercise+changed+these+7+people%27s+lives&aqs=chrome..69i57.13148j0j4&sourceid=chrome&ie=UTF-8

Manufactured by Amazon.ca
Bolton, ON